THE DESIGNFUL COMPANY

THE DESIGN COMPANY

FUL

HOW TO BUILD A CULTURE OF NONSTOP INNOVATION

A WHITEBOARD OVERVIEW BY **MARTY NEUMEIER**

THE DESIGNFUL COMPANY

HOW TO BUILD A CULTURE OF NONSTOP INNOVATION

A WHITEBOARD OVERVIEW BY MARTY NEUMEIER

NEW RIDERS
1249 EIGHTH STREET
BERKELEY, CA 94710
510/524-2178
800/283-9444
510/524-2221 (FAX)

NEW RIDERS IS AN IMPRINT OF PEACHPIT, A DIVISION OF PEARSON EDUCATION

FIND US ON THE WORLD WIDE WEB AT: WWW.PEACHPIT.COM
TO REPORT ERRORS, PLEASE SEND A NOTE TO ERRATA@PEACHPIT.COM

PROJECT EDITOR:	**PRODUCTION EDITOR:**	**INDEXER:**	**BOOK DESIGNER:**
RACHEL TILEY	LUPE EDGAR	CHERYL LENSER	CLAUDIA FUNG

ISBN 0-321-34810-9

9 8 7 6 5 4 3 2 1

PRINTED AND BOUND IN THE UNITED STATES OF AMERICA

PREFACE

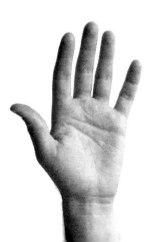

Welcome to the future of business. Whether you're the CEO of a global firm or the newest employee in a startup, the principles in these pages will help you ride powerful currents of change. It's too late to label this book a manifesto—the revolution has already begun. Instead, I hope THE DESIGNFUL COMPANY will serve as your personal guide to the challenging world of nonstop innovation.

In my first whiteboard book, THE BRAND GAP, I showed how to bridge the distance between business strategy and customer experience with five interconnected disciplines. In my second book, ZAG, I drilled down into the first and most strategic of these five disciplines, radical differentiation. Now, in THE DESIGNFUL COMPANY, I'll show you how to transform your company by unleashing the full potential of creative collaboration.

I know your time is valuable, so once again I've compressed my thoughts into an "airplane book"— a quick read designed to deliver solid insights for years to come. I'll be watching as you design an exciting future for yourself, your company, and the small community we call Earth.

—Marty Neumeier

CONTENTS

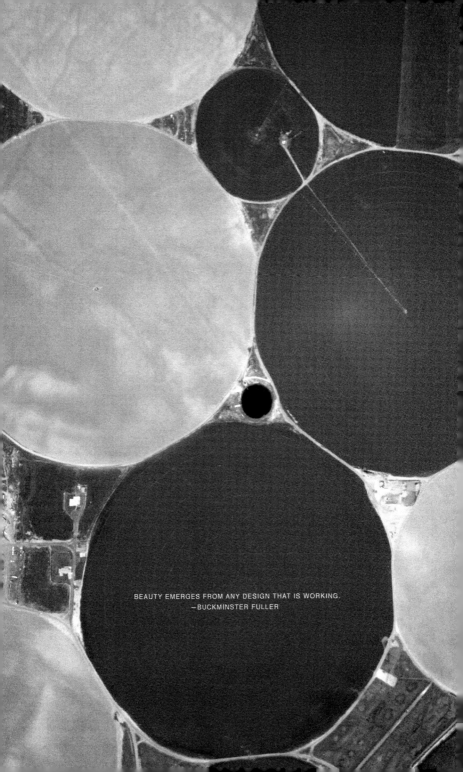

BEAUTY EMERGES FROM ANY DESIGN THAT IS WORKING.
—BUCKMINSTER FULLER

INTRODUCTION

THE AGE OF WICKED PROBLEMS.

Industrial Age thinking has delivered some dazzling capabilities, including the power to churn out high-quality products at affordable prices. Yet it has also trapped us in a tangle of what social planner Horst Rittel labeled "wicked problems"—problems so persistent, pervasive, or slippery that they seem insoluble. Unlike the relatively tame problems found in math, chess, or cost accounting, wicked problems tend to shift disconcertingly with every attempt to solve them. Moreover, the solutions are never right or wrong, just better or worse.

The world's wicked problems crowd us like piranha. You know the list: pollution, overpopulation, dwindling natural resources, global warming, technological warfare, and a lopsided distribution of power that has failed to address massive ignorance or third-world hunger. In the world of business, managers face a subset of these problems: breakneck change, omniscient customers, balkanized markets, rapacious shareholders, traitorous employees, regulatory headlocks, and pricing pressure from desperate global competitors with little to lose and everything to gain.

2008 SURVEY OF WICKED PROBLEMS*
Sponsored by Neutron and Stanford University

1 Balancing long-term goals with short-term demands

2 Predicting the returns on innovative concepts

3 Innovating at the increasing speed of change

4 Winning the war for world-class talent

5 Combining profitability with social responsibility

6 Protecting margins in a commoditizing industry

7 Multiplying success by collaborating across silos

8 Finding unclaimed yet profitable market space

9 Addressing the challenge of eco-sustainability

10 Aligning strategy with customer experience

A wicked problem is a puzzle so persistent, pervasive, or slippery that it can seem insoluble.

In a 2008 survey sponsored by Neutron and Stanford University, 1,500 top executives were asked to identify the wickedest problems plaguing their companies today. While the list included the usual suspects of profits and growth, it also revealed concerns that hadn't shown up on corporate radar screens until now: aligning strategy with customer experience, addressing eco-sustainability, collaborating across silos, and embracing social responsibility. The number-one wicked problem cited by leaders was the conflict between long-term goals and short-term demands.

Clearly, these were not the concerns of 20th-century managers. The last management obsession of the 20th century was Six Sigma, the total-quality movement inspired by Dr. W. Edwards Deming and his postwar work with the Japanese. Six Sigma has been so successful that quality has virtually become a commodity. Customers now expect every product and service to be reliable, affording no single company a competitive advantage. Unfortunately, the more progressive elements of Deming's philosophy were all but ignored by a business mindset that preferred the measurable over the meaningful.

A ONE-TRACK MIND.

When we look around and see today's companies and brands beset by distrustful customers,
disengaged employees, and suspicious communities, we can link these problems to a legacy
management style that lacks any real humanity.
The model for 20th-century management was
not the warm humanism of the Renaissance,
but the cold mechanics of the assembly line, the
laser-like focus of Newtonian science applied to
the manufacture of wealth. The assembly line
was intentionally blind to morality, emotions, and
human aspiration—all the better to make your
competitors and customers lose, so you can win.

Yet business, at bottom, is not mechanical
but human. Today we're finding that innovation
without emotion is uninteresting. Products without aesthetics are uncompelling. Brands without
meaning are undesirable. And a business without
ethics is unsustainable. The management model
that got us here is underpowered to move us

forward. To succeed, the new model must replace the win-lose nature of the assembly line with the win-win nature of the network.

In 2006, when Ford Motor announced plans to close 14 factories and cut 34,000 jobs, Bill Ford made a revealing statement: "We can no longer play the game the old way," he said. "From now on, our vehicles will be designed to satisfy the customer, not just fill a factory." Too little, too late. While Ford was figuring this out, Toyota had already been satisfying customers for years.

We've spent the last century trying to fill factories and making minor tweaks to the same basic idea of efficiency. The high-water mark in the quest for continuous improvement is Six Sigma, yet THE WALL STREET JOURNAL cited a 2006 Qualpro study showing that, of 58 large companies that have announced Six Sigma programs, 91% have trailed the S&P 500. We've been getting better and better at a management model that's getting wronger and wronger.

GO ASK ALICE.

In an era of Six Sigma sameness, it's no longer enough to get better. We have to get different. Not just different, but REALLY different. In ZAG I proposed a 17-step process to create the radical differentiation necessary for companies, products, and brands stand out from a marketplace of increasing clutter. Thanks to unprecedented market clutter, differentiation is becoming the most powerful strategy in business and the primary beneficiary of innovation.

So if innovation drives differentiation, what drives innovation? The answer, hidden in plain sight, is design. Design contains the skills to identify possible futures, invent exciting products, build bridges to customers, crack wicked problems, and more. The fact is, if you wanna innovate, you gotta design.

Imagine a crazy world where what you learned in business school is either upside down or backward—where customers control the company, jobs are avenues of self-expression, the barriers to competition are out of your control, strangers design your products, fewer features are better, advertising drives customers away, demographics are beside the point, whatever you sell you take back, best practices are obsolete at birth; where meaning talks, money walks, and stability is fantasy; where talent trumps obedience, imagination beats knowledge, and empathy trounces logic.

If you've been paying close enough attention, you don't have to imagine this Alice-in-Wonderland scenario. You see it forming all around you. The only question is whether you can change your business fast enough to take full advantage of it.

The management innovation that is destined to kick Six Sigma off its throne is design thinking. It will take over your marketing department, move into your R&D labs, transform your processes, and ignite your culture. It will create a whip action that will bring finance into alignment with creativity, and eventually reach deep into Wall Street to change the rules of investing.

IF YOU WANNA

INNOVATE,

YOU GOTTA

DESIGN.

DESIGN, DESIGN, WHERE ART THOU?

The discipline of design has been waiting patiently in the wings for nearly a century, relegated to supporting roles and stand-in parts. Until now, companies have used design as a beauty station for identities and communications, or as the last stop before a product launch. Never has it been used for its potential to create rule-bending innovation across the board. Meanwhile, the public is developing a healthy appetite for all things design.

One survey by Kelton Research found that when 7 in 10 Americans recalled the last time they saw a product they just had to have, it was because of design. They found that with younger people 18-29, the influence of design was even more pronounced. More than one out of four young adults were disappointed in the level of design in America, saying, for example, that cars were better designed 25 years ago.

In Great Britain, a recent survey commissioned by The Design Council found that 16% of British businesses say that design tops their list of key success factors. Among "rapidly growing" businesses, a whopping 47% rank it first.

The mushrooming demand for design is being shaped by a profound shift in how the first world makes its living: creativity in its various forms has become the number-one engine of economic growth. The "creative class," using the words of University of Toronto professor Richard Florida, now comprises 38 million members, or more than 30% of the American workforce. McKinsey authors Lowell Bryan and Claudia Joyce put the figure only slightly below at 25%. They cite creative professionals in financial services, health care, high tech, pharmaceuticals, and media and entertainment who act as agents of change, producers of intangible assets, and creators of new value for their companies.

When you hear the phrase innovative design, what picture comes to mind? An iPhone? A Prius? A Nintendo Wii? Most people will visualize some kind of technology product. Yet products—technological or otherwise—are not the only possibilities for design. Design is rapidly moving from "posters and toasters" to include processes, systems, and organizations.

Dr. Deming, the mid-century business guru who inspired Six Sigma, had some far-reaching ideas beyond quality control. You'd expect his thinking to be stuck in the rusty past, but it remains remarkably progressive by modern standards. His trademark 1982 "System of Profound Knowledge" was an attempt to get managers to think outside the system they're working in. It featured a list of "deadly diseases," including a lack of purpose, the mobility of executives, and an emphasis on short-term profits (sound familiar?). Among the diseases was an over-reliance on technology to solve problems.

The sure cure for Deming's diseases, as well as for the top ten wicked problems, is design. It's the accelerator for the company car, the power train for sustainable profits: design drives innovation; innovation powers brand; brand builds loyalty; and loyalty sustains profits. If you want long-term profits, don't start with technology, start with design.

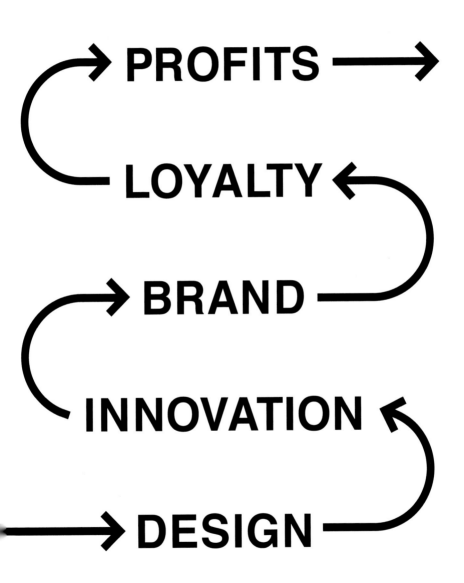

PROFITS →

LOYALTY ←

BRAND

INNOVATION ←

→ **DESIGN**

BRAND AND DELIVER.

There are really only two main components for business success: brands and their delivery. All other activities—finance, manufacturing, marketing, sales, communications, human relations, investor relations—are sub-components.

In THE BRAND GAP I defined a brand as a person's gut feeling about a product, service, or company. I showed where brands derive their financial value, drawing a distinction between me-too brands and charismatic brands. Charismatic brands support higher profit margins because their customers believe there's no substitute for them; they form unbreachable barriers to competition in an era of cut-throat pricing.

A former editor of WINDOWS magazine, Mike Elgan, illustrated the difference between ordinary brands and charismatic brands in two succinct sentences: "Microsoft CEO Steve Ballmer is famous for a crazy video in which he yells, I—LOVE—THIS—COMPANY. With Apple, it's the customers who shout that." This may explain why BusinessWeek's top-100 survey placed Microsoft's brand value at only 17% of its market cap, and Apple's at an impressive 66%.

The well-documented connection between customer loyalty and profit margins has encouraged many companies to launch so-called loyalty programs, using incentives or contracts to "lock in" customers. Trouble is, customers don't like to be locked in. It makes them disloyal. Not only that, loyalty programs are expensive to manage and easy to copy. They're nothing more than Band-aids on a much deeper problem—offerings so uncompelling that customers prefer to keep their options open.

In the previous century, a little brand loyalty went a long way. Often, what passed for loyalty was merely ignorance. If customers didn't know what their options were, they would simply stick with the devil they knew. Today's Microsoft, with its low brand score, may be one of the last major companies to profit this way. In the new century, customer ignorance won't be enough to keep competitors at bay.

To build a brand that fosters voluntary loyalty, it's better to do what Google does: Use design to create differentiated products and services that delight customers.

I'm Feeling Lucky

d × d = :D

DIFFERENCE   DESIGN   DELIGHT

If you can deliver customer delight, you can dispense with the high cost and relationship-straining effects of loyalty programs. Organic loyalty beats artificial loyalty every time.

The central problem of brand-building is getting a complex organization to execute a bold idea. It's as simple and as vexing as that. First, you have to identify and articulate the right idea. Next, you have to get hundreds or even thousands of people to act on it—in unison. Then you have to update, augment, or replace the idea as the market dictates.

Stacked against this challenge are two prevailing headwinds: the extreme clutter of the marketplace and the relentless speed of change. The antidote to clutter is a radically differentiated brand. The antidote to change is organizational agility. While agility was not a burning issue when business moved at a more leisurely pace, in 2008 it showed up as wicked problem number three. Companies now need to be as fast and adaptable as they are innovative.

AGILITY TRUMPS OWNERSHIP.

Today there's no safe ground in business. The old barriers to competition—ownership of factories, access to capital, technology patents, regulatory protection, distribution chokeholds, customer ignorance—are rapidly collapsing. In our Darwinian era of perpetual innovation, you're either commoditizing or revolutionizing.

A visible victim of change was Kodak at the turn of the new century, when its ownership of the patents, distribution channels, and dominant market share that protected its film and camera businesses became irrelevant against the steady advance of digital photography. Though Kodak could see the revolution coming a mile away, it couldn't extricate itself from its own culture— a culture based on squeezing profits from a commoditizing film business. By 2004 its share of the camera market was down to 17%, despite being the first on the scene with a digital camera 15 years earlier.

Why does change always have to be crisis-driven? Is it impossible to change ahead of the curve? What keeps companies from the continuous transformation needed to keep up with the speed of the market?

A company can't "will" itself to be agile. Agility is an emergent property that appears when an organization has the right mindset, the right skills, and the ability to multiply those skills through collaboration. To count agility as a core competence, you have to embed it into the culture. You have to encourage an enterprise-wide appetite for radical ideas. You have to keep the company in a constant state of inventiveness. It's one thing to inject a company WITH inventiveness. It's another thing to build a company ON inventiveness.

To organize for agility, your company needs to develop a "designful mind." A designful mind confers the ability to invent the widest range of solutions for the wicked problems now facing your company, your industry, your world.

"He that will not apply new remedies must expect new evils," warned Sir Francis Bacon in the Renaissance, "for time is the greatest innovator."

Amen.

NEXT, ECO-EVERYTHING.

Necessity may well be the mother of invention. But if we continue to manufacture mountains of toxic stuff, invention may soon become the mother of necessity. Our natural resources will be depleted and our planet made uninhabitable. On the top-ten list of wicked problems, eco-sustainability is number nine with a bullet. My hunch is that it will move up rapidly until it settles into the top three.

The problem with consumerism isn't that it creates desire, but that it fails to fully satisfy it. Desire is a basic human drive. But part of what we desire is to feel good about the things we buy. We yearn for "guilt-free affluence," to use the words of Worldchanging's Alex Steffen.

What does this have to do with design? Every-thing. The answers to pollution and vanishing resources will not come from politicians—they'll come from the fertile minds of scientists, research-ers, engineers, architects, planners, and entrepre-neurs, many of whom will have a profit motive.

As a thought experiment, imagine a future in which all companies were compelled to take back every product they made. How would that change their behavior? For starters, they would make their products with parts they could salvage and reuse at the end of their life cycles. This in turn would spawn whole industries dedicated to the design of reusable materials. As companies struggled to afford the full cost of manufacturing, the prices of products and services would rise. To keep prices under control, companies would localize their operations to save on transportation costs. Localizing businesses would change the nature of communities, creating a network of quasi-independent economies more akin to the Agricultural Age than the Industrial Age.

As you can see, the domino effect caused by a focus on waste reduction would alter our commercial landscape beyond recognition, creating more wicked problems, but also more opportunities.

In France, where the Agricultural Age is still in evidence, the large-scale Boisset Winery is rediscovering the value of the old ways. It's replacing heavy, diesel burning tractors with horse-drawn plows and grass-munching sheep to restore the compacted, depleted topsoil. It's also discovering value in new technologies, bucking the French tradition of corks and glass bottles by shipping its wine in recyclable Tetra Pak containers that reduce

transportation weight and manufacturing costs.

In Germany, Volkswagen is demonstrating that corporate responsibility doesn't end at the loading dock. The company is already selling cars that are 85% recyclable and 95% reusable, and building a zero-emissions car that operates on a fuel cell, 12 batteries, and a solar panel instead of fossil fuels.

The European Union has announced a "20/20 vision." It wants to get 20% of its energy from renewable sources by the year 2020. If this were to come from sun power, it would require 25 times the current annual production of solar panels to meet the need. In Silicon Valley, Applied Materials has a complementary vision: to have its equipment be used for making three-quarters of the world's solar panels by the year 2011.

American furniture manufacturer Steelcase is currently attacking the waste stream with its Think chair, which is nearly 100% fixable and recyclable.

The company has also set up three different factories around the world to lower transportation costs and support local economies.

Industrial giant General Electric once found itself in the penalty box for dumping toxic chemicals into the Hudson River. Today it spends nearly $1 billion a year on research into eco-friendly technologies to improve energy efficiency, desalinate water sources, and reduce dependence on fossil fuels. The motive? Profit. As CEO Jeffery Immelt says, "Green is green."

While eco-sustainability isn't yet top of mind for most CEOs, when the tide finally turns, it'll turn fast. There's already a significant migration of talented executives from traditional technology to green technology. As venture capitalist Adam Grosser put it, "They've had their consciousness energized, and they also believe there's a lot of money to be made."

TRADITIONAL BUSINESS IS DESIGN BLIND.
Until a decade or so ago, the public's taste for design had been stunted by the limitations of mass production. Now, people have more buying choices, so they're choosing in favor of beauty, simplicity, and the "tribal identity" of their favorite brands.

Yet if design is such a powerful tool, why aren't there more practitioners working in corporations? If economic value is increasingly derived from intangibles like knowledge, inspiration, and creativity, why don't we hear the language of design echoing through the corridors?

Unfortunately, most business managers are deaf, dumb, and blind when it comes to creative process. They learned their chops by rote, through a bounded tradition of spreadsheet-based theory. As one MBA joked, in his world, the language of design is a sound only dogs can hear.

This is illustrated by a story about railroad baron Collis P. Huntington, who visited the Eiffel Tower just after its completion. When an interviewer for a Paris newspaper asked him for a critique, he said: "Your Eiffel Tower is all very well, but where's the money in it?"

It's not that spreadsheet thinking is wrong. It's

just inadequate. A designer might have offered a completely different critique of the tower: "What a stirring symbol of achievement! From now on, people will never forget their visit to Paris." According to one estimate, more than $120 billion worth of Eiffel Tower souvenirs has been sold since 1897. The trinket business alone has been worth the investment.

The lesson of Paris has not been lost on cities like London, with its majestic London Eye, or Bilbao, with its shimmering Guggenheim Museum. Frank Gehry's design has not only captivated the world's imagination, but has catalyzed an economic turnaround for a whole region.

For businesses to bottle the kind of experiences that focus minds and intoxicate hearts, not just one time but over and over, they'll need to do more than hire designers. "They'll need to BE designers," says Roger Martin, dean of the Rotman School of Management at the University of Toronto. "They'll need to think like designers, feel like designers, work like designers."

The narrow-gauge mindset of the past is insufficient for today's wicked problems. We can no longer play the music as written. Instead, we have to invent a whole new scale.

PART 1 : THE POWER OF DESIGN

A NEW DEFINITION OF DESIGN.

Throughout the 20th century, designers developed their craft within the walls of a professional ghetto. Designer Ralph Caplan once complained that he and his colleagues were considered "exotic menials" by the captains of industry. While this was partly due to the dominance of spreadsheet thinking in business, it was helped along by the success of the German Bauhaus, in which the designer's mission was a matter of infusing industrial artifacts with the sensibilities of Modernist art. You can imagine the seductive pull of this vision on generations of designers who entered the profession, not through business schools or even design schools, but though art schools.

Thus, our shared understanding of design, enshrined in the pages of mainstream dictionaries, was essentially this: "A plan for an artifact or system of artifacts." Artifacts? Industrial leaders simply placed the whole discipline of design in a mental box labeled "posters and toasters." Later they moved it to a smaller box labeled "styling." Even as recently as last year, a CNET reviewer critiqued the Blackberry 7130C by saying, "It has a nice design, but how does it perform?"

Today we need a broader definition of design in which the key measurement is not styling but performance. As it turns out, the basis for a new definition was put forward 40 years ago by Herbert Simon, a leading social scientist and Nobel Laureate. In THE SCIENCES OF THE ARTIFICIAL he wrote: "Everyone designs who devises courses of action aimed at changing existing situations into preferred ones." Notice the careful selection of the words "everyone," "changing," and "situations." Notice the careful omission of the words "artist," "styling," and "artifacts." Neither poster nor toaster would have appeared in the illustrated margins of Simon's dictionary. He believed that design was a powerful tool for change, not just a tool for styling products and communications.

If we take Simon's description, but drop the florid language and legalistic tone, we end up with a new definition powerful enough to recast the way business does business in the 21st century: Design is change.

SIMON SAYS, BE A DESIGNER.

According to Simon, anyone who tries to improve a situation is a designer. In other words, you don't need an MFA to engage in designing. You just need to find a situation worth improving and then work through the creative process. Of course, this description perfectly fits architects, artists, composers, movie directors, engineers, and the other standard design roles, but it also applies to doctors, scientists, psychologists, police detectives, military strategists, supply chain managers, advertising planners, and facilities managers. It applies to all leaders, too, since the leading is the act of moving people from an existing situation to an improved one. Moses was a designer, in that sense, and so is the leader of every company with at least one employee.

While everyone uses design thinking in some situations, certain people are particularly suited to it. They tend to be: 1) empathetic, 2) intuitive, 3) imaginative, and 4) idealistic. Unfortunately, from a traditional business viewpoint, these traits translate to soft-hearted, illogical, scatterbrained, and mulish. So let's take a moment to look a bit deeper.

EMPATHETIC. In business, empathy can be used to understand the motivations of customers, fellow employees, partners, and suppliers, and to forge stronger emotional bonds with people. While this trait may have been a handicap in the days of win-lose customer relationships, in today's customer-centric marketplace, it's invaluable. Sales people can use it to design solutions to customer problems. Managers can use it to design high-functioning teams. Environmental designers can use it to design engaging experiences.

INTUITIVE. Intuition is a shortcut to understanding situations. The logical mind works through a problem in a linear A-B-C-D fashion, while the intuitive mind skips around in an C-B-D-A fashion, throwing in R-K-Z-P for good measure. Did I mention Q? While logical thinking is good for grounding and proving ideas, intuitive thinking is good for seeing the whole picture. Copywriters can use it to design a combination of words that will explode with meaning in readers' minds. HR specialists can use it to design recruiting programs that will strengthen the company's culture. CEOs can use it to see how the parts of a problem fit together. When you combine both of these styles—the

DESIGNER

logical and the intuitive—you get the ingredients of a capable leader.

IMAGINATIVE. Without a few scatterbrains on the payroll, innovation would never happen. New ideas come from divergent thinking, not convergent thinking. As creativity expert Edward de Bono once said, "You can't dig a new hole by digging the same one deeper." R&D engineers use imagination to design disruptive product platforms. Retail managers use it to design authentic ways to build customer loyalty. Web designers use it to design surprising and satisfying connections between ideas, activities, and resources.

IDEALISTIC. Creative personalities have been described as histrionic, headstrong, and dreamy. They're notorious for focusing on what's wrong, what's missing, or what they believe needs to change. Yet if your company's goal is to transform an existing situation into an improved one, to some extent, these are the people you'll need. For example, idealistic industrial designers are able to design better relationships between people and machines. Idealistic finance chiefs are able to design more transparent reporting frameworks. Idealistic entrepreneurs are able to design eco-driven business models.

HOW IS CREATIVE THINKING DIFFERENT?

Designing differs from other activities not only in its outcomes (Simon's preferred situations), but in the mental and physical processes that generate those outcomes. It takes place in the uncomfortable gap between vision and reality. The vision-reality gap is filled with "creative tension," a powerful source of energy for creative people. In the early days of navigation, mapmakers would mark the mysterious gaps on their charts with cheerful warnings such as, "There be dragons!" There be dragons in the vision-reality gap, and the truly creative people are those who are irresistibly drawn to do battle with them.

In its most basic form, the gap is the distance between "what is" and "what could be." Western thinking has been mostly concerned with "what is," and as a result we've gotten very good at analysis and argument. Traditional business has placed "what is" in the driver's seat, while strapping "what could be" into the kiddie seat where it can't disturb the driver. Yet imagine a capitalist society running entirely on "what is" thinking: Nothing would be ventured and nothing would be gained. Companies would look like identical cars with tiny engines and oversized brakes.

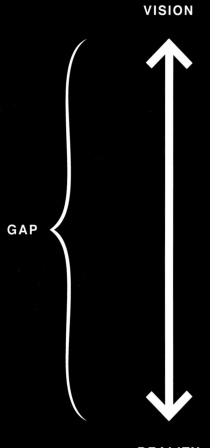

Roger Martin, dean of the Rotman School of Management, has given much thought to the differences between business reasoning and design reasoning. On the business side he puts both inductive reasoning (observing that something works) and deductive reasoning (proving that something is). On the design side he puts "abductive" reasoning (imagining that something could be). Inductive and deductive reasoning are perfect for "algorithmic" tasks with known formulas, but they're inadequate for "heuristic" tasks that deal with mysteries. Algorithmic tasks might be building a supply chain or setting prices for a new product line. Heuristic tasks might be fostering supplier relationships or understanding consumer behavior. Heuristic tasks are not governed by fixed rules, and often require steering by stars that are in constant motion.

Yet most business people are trained to take the mystery out of tasks by redefining them as familiar routines, or moving on to tasks that fit the skills they already have. If, as Martin believes, value creation in the 21st century will be about battling dragons, then business people must learn to think more like designers—masters of heuristics, not managers of algorithms.

A brief story about an advertising friend illustrates the bias against abductive reasoning. A few years ago, a client set him the task of improving the results of a direct mail campaign that had received a 1.8% response instead of the 2.1% the company had expected. My friend, in a tour de force of abductive reasoning, not only redesigned the campaign, but reinvented the whole concept of direct mail. He developed a "product story" that was sent out as a series of "chapters" over a five-week period. When the concept generated a 31% response, his clients abruptly fired him. "31% is not sustainable," they explained. They simply couldn't fit this success into their frame of reference; they thought it better to stick with incremental improvements than to deal with outcomes they couldn't predict or understand.

Fear of failure, aversion to unpredictability, preoccupation with status—these are the prime assassins of innovation. The ruthless elimination of error is one of the givens of 20th-century management. Yet error should be embraced as a necessary component of the messy, iterative, creative process. As Tom Kelley of design firm IDEO says: "It's okay to stumble as long as you fall forward."

DESIGNING THE WAY FORWARD.

The bias against abductive reasoning is unwittingly reinforced by the use of case studies in business schools. The assumption is that the answer to a given problem is contained in the specific experience of one or two companies. The fact is, the experience of one company is not always transferable to another. You can't choose a solution from the "solution shelf" as if you were buying a pair of pants from the ready-to-wear rack. In real life, you need to tailor your decisions to the unique challenge at hand, often working in dim light with incomplete measurements.

In this situation, you can't DECIDE the way forward. You have to DESIGN the way forward.

The difference between these two modes is significant. The deciding mode assumes that the alternatives already exist (in case studies), but deciding will be difficult. The designing mode assumes that new options must be imagined (using the design process), but once imagined, deciding will be easy. The truth is, success in the 21st century will depend on finding the right mixture of both of these modes.

OFF-THE-RACK SOLUTIONS
ARE INSUFFICIENT IN AN AGE OF
PERPETUAL CHANGE.

Richard Boland, a professor at the Weatherhead School of Management at Case Western University says, "The problem with managers today is that they do the first damn thing that pops into their heads." After spending months studying the design process of architect Frank Gehry, Boland concluded: "There's a whole level of reflectiveness absent in traditional management that we can find in design."

Naturally, managers who rely on the decision mode will find reasons to exclude the design mode from their thinking: "We don't have time." "Our budgets won't allow it." "The real problem is political." "Our culture is too conservative." These aren't really reasons but excuses, and they condemn a company to a future of limited choices. The traditional management model is a veritable thrift store of hand-me-down concepts, all perfectly tailored for a previous need and a previous era. The old model was innovated so long ago that those who once saw business management as a cause for revolution—Frederick Taylor, Henry Ford, Alfred Sloan, and others—are long gone. We need a new band of revolutionaries to enlarge the scope of possibilities.

In the meantime, we're seeing the breakdown of a management model so bereft of ideas that it has resorted to "unlocking" wealth through financial manipulation rather than "creating" wealth through designful innovation. Boland suggests that Enron's failure was not only a failure of ethics but a failure of imagination. Its managers engaged in hiding debt with convoluted transactions because they simply didn't have any better ideas. In many sectors, the age-old American dream of building a business has devolved to the "dream of the deal." What's missing here is the imaginative idealism of design.

The key to finding solutions to wicked problems, such as Enron's, is the designer's ability to embrace paradox—a willingness to stay in the dragon gap as long as it takes, to brave the discomfort of creative tension until the conflicting issues are resolved. This ability is conferred on all human beings, not just designers, through the evolutionary principle of bilateralism. We're all born with two eyes, two ears, two hands, and two brain hemispheres. Two eyes give us perspective. Two ears give us sound location. Two hands give us the ability to use tools. And the two sides of our brain give us the ability to grasp problems in the pincer grip of logic and intuition.

The Partners, a leading design firm in London, refers to this knack as "third brain thinking." When the left brain and right brain work together, a third brain emerges that can do what neither brain can do alone. The third brain is a metaphor for holistic thinking, and it's the perfect model for embedding a "design mind" in the culture of a corporation. Third-brain thinkers don't settle for easy options—they work as a team until they find the win-win ground among seemingly opposing sets of needs.

Third-brain thinkers have the ability to zoom out and zoom in on a problem. They zoom out to see where the problem fits in the larger scheme of things, then zoom back in to concentrate on the details. Zooming out facilitates strategic differentiation, while zooming in facilitates quality. To the third-brain thinker, business solutions that fail to combine differentiation and quality are of little interest and of questionable value. Apple's CEO Steve Jobs is the third brain personified. A few years ago, while leading his company through a minefield of competitive threats, he insisted that a shipment of Italian marble bound for Manhattan's first Apple store be held until he could inspect the veining patterns. It seems that no issue is too big and no issue is too small for the designful mind.

In the panoply of problems facing corporate leaders today, a common thread is the either-or nature of trade-offs. This is what makes wicked problems so wicked. Designful leaders don't accept the hand-me-down notion that cost-cutting and innovation are mutually exclusive, or that short-term and long-term goals are irreconcilable. They reject the tyranny of "or" in favor of the genius of "and."

Designful leaders are adrenalized by the ambiguity and uncertainty that come with constant change. They're driven to CREATE wealth instead of merely unlocking it. And they're willing to trade the false security of best practices for the insecurity of new practices. The designful leader and the creative artist are nearly one in the same. "The function of the creative artist," said composer Ferruccio Busoni, "consists of making laws, not in following laws already made."

KNOWING, MAKING, AND DOING.

Somewhere in the middle of the last century, trained designers began touting various design processes as a way to change their status from "exotic menials" to "serious professionals." A number of processes appeared, but mostly they were one-way flow charts that guided projects though a series of phases. When you stripped away the trademarked terms and customized embellishments, they came down to four basic phases: 1) discovery, 2) ideation, 3) refinement, and 4) production. This logical sequence gave comfort to business managers, since the designing could then be managed, tracked, compared, and measured like manufacturing.

Despite being steeped in serious intent, however, this sequence no more describes the creative process than a wedding describes sex. The actual creative act is much wilder. Those who insist on tidy phases inevitably produce mediocre results, because a too-orderly process rules out random inspiration. Rule-busting innovation requires a sense of play, a sense of delight, a refusal to be corralled into a strict method. Design is a "ludic" process, from the Latin LUDERE, meaning "to play."

KNOW

DO

You can't tell a designer to have an inspired idea by 9:30. Instead, the process has to "play" out while the designer bounces around in the space between logic and magic.

The easiest way to understand the design process is to see how it differs from traditional business processes. Industrial Age processes emphasize two main activities: knowing and doing. You analyze a problem relative to a standard box of options, then execute the solution. The traditional company is all head and legs. The designful company inserts a third activity: making. You analyze a problem, "make" a new set of options, then execute the solution. By inserting making between knowing and doing, you bring an entirely different way of working to the problem. The head and legs are improved by adding a pair of hands.

Yet designers don't actually "solve" problems. They "work through" them. They use non-logical processes that are difficult to express in words but easier to express in action. They use models, mockups, sketches, and stories as their vocabulary. They operate in the space between knowing and doing, prototyping new solutions that arise

KNOW

MAKE

DO

from their four strengths of empathy, intuition, imagination, and idealism.

In the making mode, designers never know what the outcome will be. Instead, they learn what they're doing while they're doing it. Systems thinker Donald Schon referred to this phenomenon as "reflection in action." He described it as a "dynamic knowing process" based on a repertoire of skilled responses rather than a body of knowledge. It goes far to explain what we mean by a practitioner's "artistry." Like the painter who discovers what the canvas will look like one brushstroke at a time, reflection in action combines thinking and doing, always in the moment, often under stress, while the train is still running. Yet this skill is not limited to professional designers. Examples of reflection in action in other professions include the doctor who responds to an anomalous set of symptoms by inventing and testing a new diagnosis. Or the banker who assesses credit risk, and while the numbers look right, something still "feels" wrong. Or the market researcher who "listens to the market" and finds a promising new use for an existing product.

The most innovative designers take it one step further. They consciously reject the standard option

box and cultivate an appetite for "thinking wrong."
At Apple Computer, star designer Jonathan Ive
says, "One of the hallmarks of the team is this
sense of looking to be wrong...because then you
know you've discovered something new."

At MavLab, a consulting firm on the edge of
the Pacific near the famed surf spot, Maverick's,
thinking wrong is their raison d'etre. They specia-
lize in getting whole groups of strategists and
executives to think wrong together. Of course, many
times thinking wrong is just wrong, but sometimes
it turns out more right than right.

Physicist Freeman Dyson believed that the
appearance of wrongness was proof of true
creativity. "When the great innovation appears, it
will almost certainly be in a muddled, incomplete,
and confusing form," he said. "For any specula-
tion which does not at first glance look crazy, there
is no hope." A company that automatically jumps
from knowing to doing will find that innovation
is unavailable to it. To be innovative, a company
needs not only the head and legs of knowing
and doing, but the intuitive hands of making.

THE ORGANIC DRIVETRAIN.

A 2007 McKinsey study looked at the performance of 1,077 companies over an 11-year period. It found that less than 1% outperformed their competitors on both revenue growth and profitability. What the top nine performers had in common were these two things: 1) a preference for organic growth over acquisitions, and 2) a heavy reliance on intangibles such as strong brands to drive performance.

Sustainable growth and profitability are not borrowed from the future by starving the flow of investment, and not squeezed from the past by milking a business model on its last legs. Sustained greatness, by definition, is sustainable. The look of sustainability can result from blind luck—stringing together a series of unrelated successes—but real sustainability results from a consciously built culture of innovation.

For example, GE chief Jeff Immelt has set the goal of becoming the world's largest growth company. Yet GE would have to add a new business as profitable as Nike every year to maintain its current rate of growth. Rather than simply acquire a company as profitable as Nike every year, GE is trying to grow organically—by redesigning core processes such as strategic planning, executive training, and financial reviews. While acquisitions may offer a temporary uptick in profitability, organic growth is the gift that keeps on giving.

Boston Consulting Group recently surveyed 940 executives who said organic growth was absolutely "essential" to their success. However, less than half were happy with the return on their R&D investment. Why? Because organic growth is like gardening. There are no fast-growth fertilizers that guarantee long-term success. Gardeners will be

happy to give you the only formula that works: "First year, sleep. Second year, creep. Third year, leap." You need to keep the garden stocked with innovations at different stages of development so that, in any given season, some are sleeping, some are creeping, and some are leaping.

When you ask CEOs what keeps them up at night, the answer is usually shareholder value.

When you ask them what drives the stock price, the answer is often earnings growth. When you ask what drives earnings growth, the answer may be innovation, or it may be a blank stare. If you probe more deeply into what drives innovation, only a few will understand that innovation comes from company culture. And when you ask what drives that, even fewer will say that visionary leadership is the key to fostering a culture of innovation.

Yet that's how organic growth works. If you want to drive the stock price higher—and sus-

CULTURE

tain it—you need to invest in vision, culture, and innovation rather than fast-growth fixes such as acquisitions, stock buy-backs, and massive ad campaigns. While these can produce short-term results, they usually stop producing as soon as you stop investing, leaving you right back where you were when you started.

McKinsey found that out of 157 companies that invested in acquisitions in the 1990s, only 12% grew faster than their peers, and only seven companies generated above-average shareholder returns. It's not that acquisitions are always bad. But they work best when they're used to fulfill vision, enrich culture, and drive innovation rather than temporarily prop up shareholder value. Many of the traditional tools that managers are using—public relations, advertising, lobbying, lawyering, and financial jiggering— are the wrong tools. They encourage short-term

INNOVATION

investment at the expense of long-term wealth.

But let's say you moved your investment back along the drivetrain, betting more heavily on innovation than on acquisitions, buy-backs, and the various tools of persuasion. What if you focused on designing great customer experiences. That's exactly what Apple has been doing, and the company's stock price has risen 1,273% over a ten-year period, beating the averages of any given tech market. When THE WALL STREET JOURNAL asked CEO Steve Jobs how Apple will stay on that trajectory, he replied, "We intend to keep innovating."

Apple can keep innovating because it has a CULTURE of innovation. The ingredients of revolution, renewal, and agility are baked in. Business history is dotted with the innovations of one-hit wonders, but innovative cultures are rare. To build an innovative culture, a company must keep itself

GROWTH

in a perpetual state of reinvention. Radical ideas must be the norm, not the exception.

Lou Gerstner, who transformed IBM in the 1990s, was an outspoken advocate of organizational culture. "Culture isn't just one aspect of the game— it IS the game," he said. "Vision, strategy, marketing, financial management—any management system, in fact—can set you on the right path and can carry you for a while. But no enterprise—whether in business, government, education, health care, or any area of human endeavor—will succeed over the long haul if those elements aren't part of its DNA."

Mergers, de-mergers, spin-offs, share buy-backs, and other keys to unlocking shareholder wealth have built-in limits. At some point you can no longer unlock wealth—you have to create it. And to create anything, especially wealth, there are no better tools than those of design thinking.

VALUE

THOUGHT LEADERSHIP

BUSINESS MODEL

ORGANIZATIONAL STRUCTURE

STRATEGIC DECISIONS

INTERNAL COMMUNICATIONS

OPERATIONAL PROCESSES

BRAND ECOSYSTEM

CUSTOMER RELATIONSHIPS

PRODUCTS AND SERVICES

EXTERNAL CONVERSATIONS

THE LADDER OF DESIGN LEVERAGE.

Where can you apply design thinking to gain the greatest advantage for your company? You can certainly use it in the traditional areas of products and communications, and you absolutely should. Design has barely scratched the surface of what's possible in R&D, industrial design, marketing communications, online advertising, and brand identity. One thing is for sure, though—the revolution will not be televised. The days of manufacturing a so-so product and forcing it into the market through mass advertising have come to an end. What will replace it? Design, including the design of networked advertising.

But what if you go up the ladder? Design can also be applied to consumer experiences such as help lines, customer service, online interaction, live events, shopping environments, wayfinding systems, and other branded elements that surround a product or service. A Bain & Co. study showed that 80% of executives think they're doing an excellent job of serving customers, but only 8% of customers agree. Smart companies are attacking this service gap with gusto. In a casual conversation I recently had with a Whole Foods employee, he confided that he wasn't really a cashier—he was an "environmental experience steward."

From the design of experiences, it's a short step up the ladder to addressing the brand ecosystem—the entire community of investors, partners, suppliers, and employees who contribute to the reputation and success of the company. To ensure an equitable and sustainable ecosystem, everyone must give something, and everyone must get something. The gives and gets can be more than an accident—they can be designed.

Further up the ladder, design thinking can be aimed at operational processes, creating new ways to streamline innovation, to apply metrics, to optimize supply chains, and a whole host of activities that help employees and partners work together more effectively.

If you want to out-innovate the competition, you first have to out-learn it. Design can be used to transform the flow of critical information, as well as to create dynamic training programs that can turn the company into a powerhouse of perpetual learning. The higher design moves up the ladder, the more leverage it delivers.

INNOVATIONINTERACTIVITYCONVERGE

COLLABORATIONEMOTIONALIN

NOMYFRICTIONLESSC

ORGANIZATIONSINTELLECT

ALIZATIONCOMPUTINGELECTRONICE

ONAGEGRAPHICALUSERI

TTINGINTELLECTUALPROPERTYG

SISSPACEEXPLORATIONLATERALTHINK

ATIONBEZIERCURVESKAIZEN

TELEVISIONBROADCASTING

HNOGRAPHYCOLLECTIVEUN

ANDBENEFITSCORPORATEIDENTITY

EPARTMENTSTORESXRAYSSK

SUTILITARIANISMDAGUERREOTYPESJ

TROMAGNETISMTHERMO

APHOREGASLIGHTINGENLIGHTENME

RIESDIDEROTSENCYCLOPEDIA

NTRYBOOKKEEPINGCIRCUM

LIGAZETTESSHORTHANDQUOT

NINGWHEELSTAINEDGLASSPRI

NPOWDERCASTIRONHU

MOSAICSMEGAPHONELIBRARIES

CMETHODILLUMINATEDMANUSCRIP

MEASUREMENTPAPERMAKIN

THEMATICSHORSEDRAWNVEHICLESHIERATICS

If design is change, then strategy is design. You can't gain a competitive advantage from carrying on with business as usual. Instead, you have to design new solutions to problems—sometimes even wicked problems—that other companies are unprepared to tackle. The conscious application of design thinking and visual prototyping not only expands the quantity and quality of strategic options, but helps decision-makers visualize and de-risk bold moves.

Bold moves will be difficult to execute unless the organizational structure is designed to facilitate them. When applied to reporting structures, collaboration models, and physical work environments, design thinking can lead to an unmatchable competitive advantage.

Design thinking can also influence your business model, or how the company makes money. If your company is a multi-product or multi-service firm, design thinking can organize and simplify your brand architecture, which in turn can take complexity out of the system and reduce the cost of inputs.

Finally, at the very top of the ladder, you can apply design thinking to the thought leadership that activates the corporate drivetrain. The company's mission, values, goals, and top-line messaging, when machined to a high tolerance by design, will accelerate the company over any number of bumps, dips, and unseen potholes.

When you survey the greatest innovations of all time, you can't help but notice that very few are products or communications. Instead, they're breakthroughs like cybernetics, mathematics, the long bow, navigation, moveable type, iron plows, and public education. At Neutron we've engraved about two hundred of these on the wall of our reception area — just to keep our sights high.

We play a little card game with our clients called "What do you really want?" It's a simple tool for prioritizing initiatives by dividing them into visionary, strategic, and tactical initiatives, then arranging them left to right on a timeline. If a client asks us to help with an analyst presentation, for example, we might say, "Okay, but what do you really want—a presentation or a lift in the stock price?"

If what you want from design is the greatest possible leverage, it always pays to move it up the ladder.

WHAT DO YOU *REALLY* WANT?

To refocus
our business

WHAT DO YOU *REALLY* WANT?

To unleash
organizational
talent

WHAT DO YOU *REALLY* WANT?

To increase
brand
differentiation

WHAT DO YOU *REALLY* WANT?

To move up
the positioning
ladder

WHAT DO YOU *REALLY* WANT?

To collaborate
more
effectively

WHAT DO YOU *REALLY* WANT?

To remodel
our brand
architecture

WHAT DO YOU *REALLY* WANT?

To develop
better tools and
processes

WHAT DO YOU *REALLY* WANT?

To invent the
next big thing

WHAT DO YOU *REALLY* WANT?

To accelerate
our growth

WHAT DO YOU *REALLY* WANT?

To build
an enduring
company

WHAT DO YOU *REALLY* WANT?

To discover
untapped
market space

THE RIGHT QUESTIONS
CAN HELP COMPANIES THINK
ABOUT WHAT THEY
REALLY WANT.

WHAT DO YOU *REALLY* WANT?

To build a
barrier to
competition

WHAT DO YOU *REALLY* WANT?

To launch a
persuasive ad
campaign

WHAT DO YOU *REALLY* WANT?

To establish a
brand education
program

PART 2 : THE REBIRTH OF AESTHETICS

A LANGUAGE FOR THE SENSES.

I'm not a big fan of the 13th-century philosopher Thomas Aquinas, but I have to admit, when I first read, "Ad pulcritudenum tria requiruntur integritas, consonantia, claritas," I was right there with him. Roughly translated, he was saying beauty requires three qualities: integrity, harmony, and radiance. Integrity is the quality of standing out clearly from the background. Harmony is how the parts relate to the whole. Radiance refers to the pleasure we feel when we experience it. And the language of beauty, according to Aristotle, is aesthetics.

But what does aesthetics have to do with 21st-century business? Didn't all that stuff die out with the Medici? Isn't strategy more powerful than beauty? Not so fast. An idea is only an intention until it's been perfected, polished, and produced. While design thinking can deliver the raw horsepower needed for innovation, design execution is where the rubber meets the road. Aesthetics gives us a toolbox for beautiful execution.

Some modern philosophers claim that beauty is universal, connecting our senses with deep evolutionary tides. Others say it's associative, drawing its power from ephemeral signals. I believe it's both.

There are shapes, sounds, scents, juxtapositions, and patterns that push our emotional buttons no matter who we are, where we live, or what we believe in. And there are others that shift with each person's viewpoint or situation. The round proportions of a baby's face hold appeal for all of us, but the round proportions of VW Beetle may only hold appeal to those who belong to the Beetle tribe.

Of course, everyone knows you can apply the principles of aesthetics to the curve a fender, the typography of a web page, or the textures in a clothing line. Yet you can also apply them to upstream strategy, organizational change, and marketplace reputation. For example, when you increase differentiation, you're actually using the principle of integrity. When you optimize synergy, you're using harmony. And when you enhance customer experience, you're using radiance.

Most people would agree that there's beauty in a well-run business. But I'll go one step further: The same principles that activate other forms of art will soon be essential to the art of management. Why? Because the more technological our culture becomes, the more we'll need the sensual and metaphorical power of beauty.

THE AESTHETICS OF MANAGEMENT

CONTRAST	How can we differentiate ourselves?
DEPTH	How can we succeed on many levels?
FOCUS	What should we **NOT** do?
HARMONY	How can we achieve synergy?
INTEGRITY	How can we forge the parts into a whole?
LINE	What is our trajectory over time?
MOTION	What advantage can we gain from speed?
NOVELTY	How can we use the surprise element?
ORDER	How should we structure our organization?
PATTERN	Where have we seen this before?
REPETITION	Where are the economies of scale?
RHYTHM	How can we optimize time?
PROPORTION	How can we keep our strategy balanced?
SCALE	How big should our business be?
SHAPE	Where should we draw the edges?
TEXTURE	How do the details enliven our culture?
UNITY	What is the higher-order solution?
VARIETY	How can diversity drive innovation?

BEAUTY IN NATURE IS NEVER ARBITRARY.

Renowned architect Moshe Safdie noted that, in nature, beauty is a by-product of function. The color and shape of a flower is derived from its need to attract insects. The color and structure of an insect is derived from its need to camouflage itself against flowers.

Often what makes a thing beautiful is our appreciation of its benefits. The blue sky is beautiful because it promises clean air. A muscular body is beautiful because it signals good health. An oak tree is beautiful because it offers shade, shelter, and food. By the same token, an Aston Martin is beautiful because it offers aerodynamic efficiency. An Aeron chair is beautiful because it offers exceptional comfort. Einstein's relativity theory is beautiful because it offers profound simplicity.

We ascribe beauty to things we admire, then we begin to admire other things that exhibit the same beauty. At first the Aeron chair was scoffed at for its "weird" look. Later, when its look became identified with comfort, people began to find it beautiful, and less discriminating people began seeking the same look in knock-off chairs, expect-

THE REBIRTH OF AESTHETICS

ing to get the same comfort—and the same status—for a lower price. We often use beauty as a proxy for quality.

Buckminster Fuller once said, "When I'm working on a problem, I never think about beauty. But when I have finished, if the solution is not beautiful, I know it is wrong." In mathematics, Poincare could judge the quality of a solution solely on its aesthetic elegance. Software developers can spot a great algorithm by the shape and efficiency of its coding lines. There's ample evidence of mathematical beauty in nature, too, including the breathtaking complexity of fractals, the surprising consilience of theories across disciplines, and the ancient sacred ratios of geometry.

Take the Fibonacci sequence. The formula is like a children's game: Each number in the sequence is the sum of the previous two, giving you a progression that looks like 1, 1, 2, 3, 5, 8, 13, 21, 34, and so on. In nature, this progression shows up in the patterns of pine cones and palm trees. It shows up in artichoke leaves and broccoli florets. It shows up in the shapes of nautilus shells, whose walls spiral outward according to the same laws.

BEAUTY IS A SIGN OF
EXTREME EFFICIENCY
IN THE NATURE-INSPIRED
PRODUCTS OF PAX.

A company called the Pax Group has borrowed Fibonnaci geometry to reinvent the shape fan blades. Guess what? Their fan blades are 15-35% more energy efficient and 50-75% quieter. This is beauty with its sleeves rolled up.

Writing in his notebook, Leonardo da Vinci said that we "will never discover an invention more beautiful, easier, or more economical than nature's...In her inventions nothing is wanting and nothing is superfluous."

Biomimicry expert Janine Benyus explains that nature designs its products using very few materials. Instead, it uses shape to create function. She notes that any natural material that looks like plastic is one of five simple polymers. Organisms are hungry for these polymers, so they go back into the ground cycle easily. In the manufacturing world, by contrast, we use 350 complex polymers, which why recycling is so difficult. "The design challenge," she says, "is to learn how to shape them."

Klipsch Audio Technologies designs horn-loaded loudspeakers that draw inspiration from the shape of the human ear. This approach has led to speakers that can accurately produce both soft and loud sounds, produce a highly directional sound pattern, deliver unaccented bass, mid-range and treble ranges, and are highly efficient. Founder Paul Klipsch often said, "Quality is directly proportionate to efficiency."

Simplicity and efficiency are twin threads that run through the discipline of aesthetics. All living things have an instinct to economize. The efficient use of energy, materials, and food are the best defense against entropy, the tendency for all systems to lose energy. Since aesthetics is reinforced by simplicity and efficiency, it offers a powerful tool for thriving in an era of diminishing natural resources.

"It's amazing to watch the design mind work," says Benyus. "I can tell you how life works, and then a designer will take it and remake the world."

THE TINY HAIRS
ON GECKO FOOTPADS
LED TO THE DESIGN
OF REUSABLE
SUPER-ADHESIVES.

WHAT IS GOOD DESIGN?

This is the question that has haunted the design community for decades. Whenever the conversation comes up, the "eye of the beholder" argument shuts it down. Someone says that good design is design that "works," and someone else adds that the arbiter of "what works" is the individual user. At this point everyone nods and the conversation ends. But the question is never fully put to rest.

I believe there's a more universal answer. It's this: Good design does not depend so much on the eye of the beholder, but on a combination of aesthetics and ethics. Good design exhibits virtues. What virtues? You know, good old-fashioned virtues like generosity, courage, diligence, honesty, substance, clarity, curiosity, thriftiness, and wit. By contrast, bad design exhibits human vices like selfishness, fear, laziness, deceit, pettiness, confusion, apathy, wastefulness, and stupidity.

In other words, we want the same things from design that we want from our fellow humans. When we combine ethical virtues with aesthetic virtues, we get good design. The ancient Greeks framed this ideal in the context of knowing, making, and doing: "To know truth. To make beauty.

To do good." Apple's Steve Jobs framed it this way: "Design is the soul of a man-made creation."

Soul, like beauty, is one of those evanescent qualities that disappears under the microscope, but it's clearly visible when you meet it on the street. It's a quality that's been missing in a 20th-century business tradition that overvalues narrow, short-term success, and undervalues broad, long-term success. Sumantra Ghoshal, a global business leader and author, called corporate business "under-socialized and one-dimensional." He said that traditional management has only led to resentful customers, dispirited employees, and a divided society.

Why would this change? Because it has to. In an era when customers are not only omnipotent but omniscient, when over-production leads to an ecological box canyon, a selfish focus on the bottom line is bad design. Good design, in contrast, is a new management model that deliberately includes a moral dimension. It's a model that not only serves shareholders but employees, customers, partners, and communities. For the first time since the Industrial Age, successful businesses will be designful businesses.

DESIGNING IN DEPTH.

Any leader wishing to build a modern company could do worse than study an earlier company called Lord Chamberlain's Men. Its CEO, William Shakespeare, took full advantage of an aesthetic principle known as depth. By designing entertainment products that worked on multiple levels, he was able increase not only the number of customers but their satisfaction, so that they came back again and again.

Shakespeare addressed every segment of his audience in turn, from the royals sitting in the top-tier boxes to the groundlings standing in the ale-and-urine-soaked sawdust. His dialogue shifted rhythmically from high philosophy to low humor; his scenes alternated between soliloquies and sword fights; his characters represented the full range of society. Did this strategy produce profits? Methinks it did. By the end of his career he had the most successful acting company in London.

The principle of depth can be applied to any company. The opposite page shows how each part of a business, from the internal vision to the external brand, can address multiple tiers of understanding. If meaning is the new money, then depth is king.

VISION

THE CORE ELEMENTS
OF THE BUSINESS,
INCLUDING ITS
PURPOSE, MISSION,
VALUES, AND
STRATEGIES.

IDENTITY

THE SYMBOLS
THAT EXPRESS THE
COMPANY'S VISION,
INCLUDING ITS
VOICE, ITS VISUAL
PRESENTATION, ITS
PERSONALITY, AND
ITS CHARACTER.

CULTURE

THE WAY THE
COMPANY WORKS
TOGETHER,
INCLUDING ITS
PROCESSES,
ORGANIZATIONAL
STRUCTURE,
RELATIONSHIPS,
AND LANGUAGE.

PRODUCTS

THE PRODUCTS,
SERVICES, AND
EXPERIENCES
THAT GIVE THE
COMPANY ITS
COMPETITIVE
ADVANTAGE.

BRANDS

THE BEHAVIORS AND
COMMUNICATIONS
THAT CONVERT
VISION, IDENTITY,
CULTURE, AND
PRODUCTS INTO
CUSTOMER VALUE.

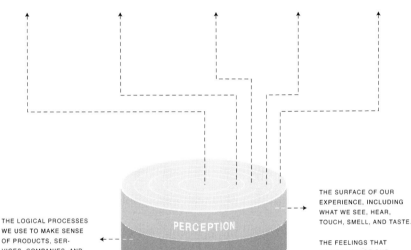

THE LOGICAL PROCESSES
WE USE TO MAKE SENSE
OF PRODUCTS, SER-
VICES, COMPANIES, AND
COMMUNICATIONS.

THE INTUITION THAT
A RELATIONSHIP WITH
A GIVEN COMPANY,
PRODUCT, OR OFFER
IS "RIGHT" FOR US.

PERCEPTION

REASON

EMOTION

RESONANCE

IDEOLOGY

THE SURFACE OF OUR
EXPERIENCE, INCLUDING
WHAT WE SEE, HEAR,
TOUCH, SMELL, AND TASTE.

THE FEELINGS THAT
DRIVE MANY OF OUR
DECISIONS, INCLUDING
THOSE THAT ARE
HIDDEN BENEATH
OUR REASON.

THE TRIBAL CONNECTION
WE FEEL WITH A BRAND—
THE DEEP KNOWLEDGE
THAT WE "BELONG" TO
ITS COMMUNITY.

DEEP DESIGN

PART 3 : LEVERS FOR CHANGE

A FLYWHEEL OF INNOVATION.

The corporate mission-scape is crowded with platitudes: "Our number-one goal is innovation." "Our vision is to develop innovative solutions." "Innovation is our only business." Unfortunately, you can't simply stick "innovation" in your tagline and expect magic to ensue. If you want to innovate, you have to build a CULTURE of innovation.

With the efficiency of a flywheel, a culture of innovation builds momentum with very small inputs, but can release large amounts of stored energy when needed. A culture of innovation combines a deep bench with a lightning response time.

Of course, it's one thing to build a company from scratch on this principle. But how do you transform a going concern? The secret is to work the leverage points. In this part of the book I'll share some of the levers we've used with our clients to launch them on a trajectory of change. Since every company is different, I'll keep the descriptions general enough to leave room for interpretation. And while I've numbered the levers from 1 to 16, this doesn't mean they must be used in a specific order. Neither does it mean that every company must use all 16 to create a shift.

LEVER 1: TAKE ON WICKED PROBLEMS

Tony Schwartz founded his firm The Energy Project on an interesting promise: Energy, not time, is our most powerful resource. Individuals and organizations can expand their energy, but they can't expand their time. Therefore, a leader must become a steward of organizational energy.

Okay, but how? Well, you might start by painting a vision so beguiling and inclusive that it rivets the attention of everyone in the company. You might then call for bold solutions to the wicked problems that stand in its way—especially problems that other companies have been too timid to tackle. You might also reward the behavior you want by giving visible support to employees and teams who align their actions with the vision.

A compelling core idea of what the company stands for can inspire a surprising amount of passion. When people have big enough goals, they tend to blow right by the little problems. The result is a culture that releases latent talent and constantly exceeds its own expectations.

FORTUNE's "100 Best Companies to Work For" recently named Google number one. In fact, the company receives over a hundred applicants for every position. Why? Because of the free lunches? The day care? The stock options? Not likely, because many others on the list offer similar perks. Instead, it's because of Google's lofty vision. When employees are asked to help "organize the world's information and make it universally accessible and useful," hearts beat a little faster. Financial enticements and office perquisites pale beside the soul-stirring goal of a race to the moon.

Now let's look at what happens when a company "under-envisions" its future. General Motors, one of the biggest successes of the last century, had the technology to make hybrid cars at the same time that Toyota did. Thanks to a "can't do" culture, product leaders were afraid to approach the board with a program they knew would cost hundreds of millions of dollars. "In the end," said product chief Bob Lutz, "it cost us much more than that. It cost us our reputation for technology leadership and innovation." What happened is that they devalued their brand to protect their jobs. Theirs was culture of fear, not joyful creation, where latent talent stayed latent.

According to Robert Reich, former U.S. Secretary of Labor and author of SUPERCAPITALISM, the job of leadership is to help people overcome denial and cynicism so they can "close the gap between the ideal and reality." This is the self-same "dragon gap," the creative space between "what could be" and "what is." The leader who can articulate a compelling vision gives people the courage to create.

It turns out that painting a vivid picture of the future is a pure design problem. When you infuse a vision with design thinking, you use "making" skills to discover and illustrate a wider set of options. You begin designing the way forward instead of merely deciding the way forward.

Companies don't fail because they choose the wrong course—they fail because they can't imagine a better one. Unimaginative leaders reach for a vision from the ready-made rack, then wonder why their leadership has no followship. Few people feel inspired by the safe and the easy. Starbucks founder Howard Schultz put it this way: "Who wants a dream that's near-fetched?" If your goal is to outperform the competition from day one, dream large.

LEVER 2: WEAVE A RICH STORY

While revolution must be led from the top, it rarely starts at the top. The spirit of revolution already exists in the hearts and minds of motivated employees and loyal customers. It shows up in the individual stories that employees tell about the work they do. And it shows up in the individual stories that customers tell about the products they love. Often a leader need only act as a kind of managing editor, shaping the stories to align with a shared vision.

To make the best use of this lever, all the little stories you tell about your company and its products should add up to one big story. For example, if you were to add up all the stories told about Mini Cooper, you would have one big story entitled "Let's Motor." Very few of the stories told by the company—or its customers—would be out of alignment with this main story. In two succinct words, Mini has captured the shared vision for the brand, which combines tribal inclusiveness and focused differentiation.

When JetBlue crafted its brand vision, it used a rich mix of witty sound bites to differentiate itself from the traditional carriers. It delivered these sound bites using "free media"—the instructional cards in the seat-back pockets, the touch screens on the check-in kiosks, and the seat-selection page of the website that clearly showed the extra legroom that only JetBlue was willing to offer. Callers who were lucky enough to be put on hold were treated to a shaggy-dog story about being put on hold: "Don't think of it as being put on hold," intoned a comforting voice, "think of it as being held." It went on to innumerate, with increasing hilarity, all the joys of being held. Customers who WEREN'T put on hold began asking to BE put on hold.

When you added up all these sound bites, what you got was one big story: An airline with an unusual focus on passenger delight. This big story became the filter for every decision the company makes.

Stories seem to rise uncontrollably from a our desire to explain and share human experience. Yet some stories are "catchier" than others. In MADE TO STICK, authors Chip and Dan Heath give numerous examples of stories that cling to our brains like burrs on a Corgi. Some of the most instructive are urban legends, since they've proven to be the stickiest stories of all. What gives them their Velcro-like adhesion? According

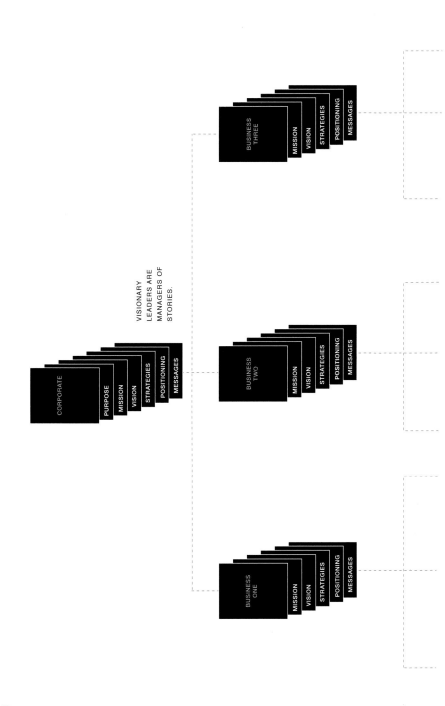

CORPORATE

PURPOSE
MISSION
VISION
STRATEGIES
POSITIONING
MESSAGES

VISIONARY
LEADERS ARE
MANAGERS OF
STORIES.

BUSINESS
THREE

MISSION
VISION
STRATEGIES
POSITIONING
MESSAGES

BUSINESS
TWO

MISSION
VISION
STRATEGIES
POSITIONING
MESSAGES

BUSINESS
ONE

MISSION
VISION
STRATEGIES
POSITIONING
MESSAGES

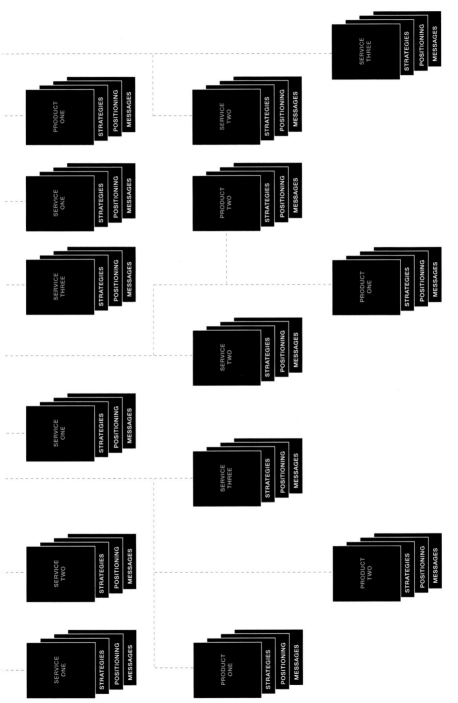

91

to the authors, it's because they're 1) simple, 2) unexpected, 3) concrete, 4) credible, and 5) emotional. When you apply these five principles to stories that align with your key messages, you deepen the emotional bond between your customers and your company.

When JetBlue launched its first long-haul route from New York to California, it faced a sudden problem. Its high-comfort-low-fare business model wouldn't permit the traditional food service. Marketing VP Amy Curtis was given a meager budget of one dollar per passenger to solve this problem. Rather than hand out a rock-hard white bagel, a slice of lunch meat, and a Tootsie Roll, she decided to tell a story. Each cross-country passenger received an airline deli bag that contained—surprise!—a T-shirt. On the front was a picture of a chicken with the headline: "Nature never meant it to fly." On the back it said: "Comfy leather seats, free DirecTV, low fares. No rubber chicken." People got it. The media loved it. And the JetBlue brand took off.

Let's compare this storytelling success against the Heath brothers' checklist. 1) Simple? Check. 2) Unexpected? Double check. 3) Concrete? Sure,

because of the rubber chicken. 4) Credible? You bet, because everyone knows they pay for airline food one way or another. 5) Emotional? Absolutely—feelings of relief, delight, and vengeful satisfaction tumble over one another as we recall the many "prison meals" we've endured in the cramped, humorless, expensive cabins of competing airlines.

Yet other stories can arise from outside the company, and these are not always flattering. In 2007, a severe winter ice storm disrupted JetBlue's flight schedules on the eve of a busy holiday week-end, causing missed flights, lost luggage, long lines, and telephone delays that even a humorous on-hold message couldn't fix. Customers and the media were not kind. The blogosphere was alive with hor-ror stories that undermined the customer-centric brand that JetBlue had worked so hard to build.

The reaction of other airlines might have been to shift the blame. After all, the weather is not within anyone's control. Yet CEO David Neeleman surprised his customers with a message that was simple, unexpected, concrete, credible, and emotional: He took complete responsibility. Within days he sent an email to every customer, placing the blame for the mishap entirely on the airline's shoulders. He said, "Words cannot express how truly sorry we are for the anxiety, frustration, and inconvenience that we caused. This is especially saddening because JetBlue was founded on the promise of bringing humanity back to air travel and making the experience of flying happier and easier for everyone who chooses to fly with us." He then announced a concrete, credible remedy— the JetBlue Airways Customer Bill of Rights.

At the bottom of the email, customers could click to see a video of Neeleman offering a sincere, emotion-laden apology. The media storm died down almost as quickly as the ice storm. JetBlue not only quelled a customer uprising, but used free spotlight time to add to its tapestry of stories and strengthen the bonds of customer loyalty.

Dear JetBlue Customers,

We are sorry and embarrassed. But most of all, we are deeply sorry.

Last week was the worst operational week in JetBlue's seven year history. Following the severe winter ice storm in the Northeast, we subjected our customers to unacceptable delays, flight cancellations, lost baggage, and other major inconveniences. The storm disrupted the movement of aircraft, and, more importantly, disrupted the movement of JetBlue's pilot and inflight crewmembers who were depending on those planes to get them to the airports where they were scheduled to serve you. With the busy President's Day weekend upon us, rebooking opportunities were scarce and hold times at 1-800-JETBLUE were unacceptably long or not even available, further hindering our recovery efforts.

Words cannot express how truly sorry we are for the anxiety, frustration and inconvenience that we caused. This is especially saddening because JetBlue was founded on the promise of bringing humanity back to air travel and making the experience of flying happier and easier for everyone who chooses to fly with us. We know we failed to deliver on this promise last week.

We are committed to you, our valued customers, and are taking immediate corrective steps to regain your confidence in us. We have begun putting a comprehensive plan in place to provide better and more timely information to you, more tools and resources for our crewmembers and improved procedures for handling operational difficulties in the future. We are confident, as a result of these actions, that JetBlue will emerge as a more reliable and even more customer responsive airline than ever before.

Most importantly, we have published the JetBlue Airways Customer Bill of Rights—our official commitment to you of how we will handle operational interruptions going forward—including details of compensation. I have a video message to share with you about this industry leading action.

You deserved better—a lot better—from us last week. Nothing is more important than regaining your trust and all of us here hope you will give us the opportunity to welcome you onboard again soon and provide you the positive JetBlue Experience you have come to expect from us.

Sincerely,

David Neeleman
Founder and CEO
JetBlue Airways

LEVER 3: ESTABLISH AN INNOVATION CENTER

Stories can be powerful building blocks for culture. So can brand guidelines, process manuals, design standards, training videos, photo libraries, talent directories, collaborative spaces, blogs, and many other internal assets.

To create a lever for change, though, you'll need to organize these assets into an innovation center—also known as a design center, or brand center. The most practical place to establish it is on the company intranet so that the tools are within easy reach of everyone. I find it helpful to think of an innovation center is a toolkit wrapped in a magazine. The tools are the ideas, formulas, processes, shortcuts, design elements, graphics, slides, training modules and other shared assets. The magazine contains the stories, case studies, blogs, and other items designed to inspire creativity and excellence. When all these assets are organized, designed, and linked, they have the power to transform the company into a sinuous creative unit.

Design is a key input here. Most intranet sites fail because they don't compete on a pair with other forms of media. People have choices, and they tend to choose "easy" over "difficult" and "attractive" over "ugly."

The Information Age has been hailed as the successor to the Industrial Age. But the true gift of digital invention is not information. It's collaboration. The ability to multiply talent by working in teams is at the core of continuous innovation. In many large companies, there are more than 10,000 professionals who contribute to innovation and brand-building. These 10,000 can account for up to 50 million collaborative relationships. As the number of professionals grows, the number of links grows exponentially, making collaboration a key leverage point.

We've barely scratched the surface of how intranet sites can mediate the process of working together, so those who master this lever can take an early lead in the race to wield culture as a competitive weapon.

Most companies generate a steady stream of quotidian design materials—products, print communications, websites, signage, retail environments, packaging, trade show exhibits, advertising, manuals, financial reports—the "toasters and posters" of the 20th-century. When you add the list of emerging opportunities—customer experience, wayfinding, service design, operational processes, branded training, organizational design, decision making, business strategy, and thought leadership—you begin to appreciate the need for strong design management.

But before you can think about building an in-house design capability, you'll need to address the problem that has plagued internal design departments since the days of the cave painters. It can be reduced to seven letters: R—E—S—P—E—C—T. As soon as a designer is hired, the perceived value of his or her talents depreciates faster than a showroom BMW. Within months the new hire will be inundated with low-level tasks and excluded from high-level conversations.

Why this happens could be the subject of another book, so for the sake of brevity I'll cut to the solution. The cure for vanishing value is to re-imagine the internal design function as an independent design studio. Since respect comes from a combination of performance and proactivity, mimicking a successful design studio can trigger the same level of respect usually reserved for external firms. Drawing on my experience at Neutron, I can offer three tips for making this transition:

1. COMPETE WITH THE OUTSIDE. Instead of expecting work to come in automatically, the internal team can adopt a more Darwinistic approach by developing skills that rival those of external firms. It can develop its own engagement processes, seek interesting problems to solve, and make "pitches" to internal clients. Like an external firm, it can prove its competence through performance metrics and design competitions. According to David Baker, a leading design management consultant, "Money is the currency of respect." He recommends instituting a charge-back system, placing a dollar value on the department's services.

And while traditional advertising is crumbling, the rules for selling online are still set in Jell-O. In-house departments may find a crucial role in mediating this conversation. Should we invest our

RESPECT IS THE FIRST CASUALTY
OF INTERNAL DESIGN TEAMS.

budget in a mobile messaging campaign, or a music video service? Should we place our bets on search advertising, or on a banner-ad series? Who knows? Questions like these will baffle marketers for years until the unknowns finally become knowns. In the meantime, it's a jump ball, so why not take a swipe at it?

2. OFFER THOUGHT LEADERSHIP. Using the Darwinistic model, not all company projects will come through the design department. That's good. First of all, not all projects are equally important. Second, there are times when the design department doesn't have the bandwidth to pay sufficient attention to a project. And finally, project owners may simply want work outside the system. As Yogi Berra put it: "If they don't want to come along, you can't stop 'em." At HP, for example, design decisions are controlled by the business heads. Says corporate design chief Sam Lucente, "It's all about persuasion." He and his team make their best case for design, then let the deciders decide.

While the role of design manager is important, the role of design persuader may be even more important. What if the internal design department could jumpstart design thinking by running educational programs on innovation, design thinking, and brand-building? The company that spreads the gospel fastest wins.

3. KNOCK DOWN THE WALLS. There's a reason design studios look the way they do: they work better that way. While tip number three may seem trivial after the first two, you'll find that by knocking down the walls of your department—both physically and figuratively—you'll clear a wide path for creative collaboration. Open spaces and high ceilings can quickly begin to unleash, unlock, and de-cube your company's talent. In fact, it's not a bad idea to extend this privilege to the rest of the company. In the no-collar workplace of the 21st century, the inspirational value of an open, creative environment cannot be overestimated.

So let's say you've re-imagined your design department as an independent studio. You've acquired design management skills, built a core team of smart design thinkers, developed a professional process for engaging with internal clients, gained a reputation for thought leadership, and knocked down the walls to invite a higher level of creative collaboration. Respect is yours. Now you're ready for the next big challenge.

LEVER 5: ASSEMBLE A METATEAM

In my first book, THE BRAND GAP, I made the case for building an integrated marketing team, or metateam. The concept of a metateam is both compelling and daunting. It proposes that the best way to manage large-scale creativity is by 1) hiring best-of-breed specialists, and 2) getting those specialists to work together as a single team. A metateam, therefore, is a team of teams.

It's fairly clear how a best-of-breed specialist or specialist team can be effective in executing a creative project. It's less clear how to get a whole metateam working together toward a larger goal.

The problem is that 20th-century business has been a training ground for non-collaboration. Companies have routinely rewarded employees, departments, and external firms for independent achievement. Schools have done the same, making collaboration look like a form of cheating. This may well account for the "Lone Ranger" model of creativity we all grew up with. It was exemplified by larger-than-life figures such as Frank Lloyd Wright, Pablo Picasso, and Sigmund Freud— people who tended to regard their peers not as collaborators but as competitors.

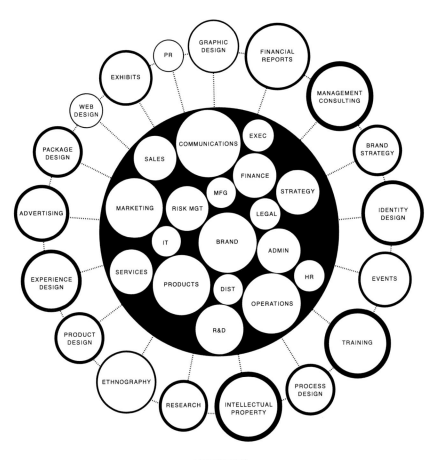

A METATEAM IS
THE MODEL OF CHOICE FOR
ADVANCED CREATIVITY.

The benefits of reversing the Lone Ranger model are substantial. A high-performing metateam can turn an organization into a coherent, agile, muscular entity. It can raise innovation and lower costs. It can be scaled up or down at a moment's notice.

As it turns out, we have plenty of exemplars to set against the lone genius view of creativity, including Hollywood's dream factories, Kennedy's space program, Edison's industrial lab, and others. In fact, the closer you look the history of design, the more you see that the lone genius is more myth than fact.

If the future of corporate design depends on the metateam, then the critical role of the internal design department is to manage it. And, like brand management, design management should NEVER be outsourced. It needs to remain strong and consistent through various strategy shifts, reorganizations, and changes in leadership.

Conversely, many of the design skills needed to execute brand-related projects should ALWAYS be outsourced, since the outside is where you find best-of-breed specialists. Possible exceptions to this rule are companies whose primary business is design, such as fashion houses, movie studios,

publishers, and advertising agencies. Yet even for design-focused companies, some or all of the design can be outsourced, as long as the design strategy remains inside. P&G has recently redefined its R&D as "C&D," or "connect and develop," so it can benefit from a wider pool of independent inventors. The company now expects half of its new products to come FROM their own labs, and the other half to come THROUGH them. In 2004, the late management expert Peter Drucker took a more extreme stance. He said that companies should outsource every role that doesn't lead to senior management.

It's unlikely that an internal creative department will ever beat the outside experts at their own game, especially over time. The free market gives powerful incentives for specialists to acquire deep-domain experience in their practice areas. Yet the internal creative department has its own deep-domain experience—knowledge of the company itself—that enables it to act as the orchestrator of the metateam effort, keeping internal and external teams focused on shared goals, and on integrating all the elements into the long-range vision.

EVEN THE LONE RANGER
DIDN'T WORK ALONE.

LEVER 6: COLLABORATE CONCERTINA-STYLE

Lest it seem that creative collaboration is a constant round of "Cum-ba-ya," let me state for the record that metateams are strictly for grownups. Prima donnas, classroom bullies, and nervous nellies need not apply. Teamwork is an advanced form of creativity, requiring players who are humble, generous, and independent-minded.

How do you get a bunch of independent-minded professionals to play nice together? By establishing sensible rules of engagement. At Neutron we've discovered that strong-willed people love to collaborate when there's a sharp delineation of roles, an unobstructed view of the goal, and a strong commitment to quality. Conversely, they hate to collaborate if they believe their work will be mitigated by pettiness, confusion, and low expectations.

Creativity can be exercised in two manners: team creativity and individual creativity. The key is finding a collaborative rhythm that incorporates both. A good rhythm looks a bit like playing the concertina, alternating between expression and impression—working separately, then working together. When small teams or individuals work separately (expression), they bring deep experience to bear. When they work together (impression), they expose their opinions to a wider view. By working back and forth from expression to impression, the result is not compromise but addition. The sum of each session is a measurable leap in shared thinking.

The primary tool for creative collaboration—and one that's under-employed today—is the design brief. A well conceived brief can focus collaborators on the common goal, reduce the costs of orientation, allocate roles and responsibilities, and provide a framework for metrics.

Yet no design brief, whether it guides, steers, or dictates, can address the psychology of human interaction. How do you navigate the treacherous waters of clashing opinions, narrow viewpoints, secret feelings, and asynchronous aspirations as you strive for consensus in a large group?

LEVER 7: INTRODUCE PARALLEL THINKING

Here's some cutting-edge advice from a management guru: "Contentious problems are best solved not by imposing a single point of view at the expense of all others, but by striving for a higher-order solution that integrates the diverse perspectives of all relevant constituents." Peter Drucker again? No. Drucker's guru, Mary Parker Follett. Follett was born at the end of the Civil War. She attended Radcliffe (before it became Radcliffe), then ran a number of successful service organizations in Boston during the early century. In 1924 she wrote a book called CREATIVE EXPERIENCE, in which she pointed out, "Adversarial, win-lose decision-making is debilitating for all concerned." Unfortunately, win-lose decision-making was—and still is—the dominant mode of business.

A common problem with collaboration is that otherwise smart, well meaning people disrupt the creative flow by disagreeing. This is not a habit we invented, but one we inherited. The Greeks, including Aristotle, Socrates, and Plato, believed that sound thinking came from discussion rather than dialogue—from finding flaws in the others' arguments rather than advancing a concept together.

WHITE
FACTUAL
AND
INFORMATIVE

RED
EMOTIONAL
AND
INTUITIVE

BLACK
CONTRARY
AND
CAUTIOUS

YELLOW
SUNNY
AND
POSITIVE

GREEN
FRESH
AND
CREATIVE

BLUE
COOL
AND
CONTROLLED

SIX THINKING HATS

After a couple thousand years of beating each other up with our personal viewpoints, creativity expert Edward de Bono has found a way to circumvent the "Gang of Three" and show people how to work through problems constructively. Called parallel thinking, it gets everyone in the group to think in the same direction at the same time, thereby neutralizing our Socratic habit of shooting down ideas before they can fly.

De Bono's book, SIX THINKING HATS, demonstrates the six ways a group can think as it works through an issue or opportunity. The "hats" are simply metaphors for different ways of getting at problems. Here's a brief overview:

The WHITE HAT represents information. What do we know about this issue? What are the facts, figures, and other data that can guide our work?

The RED HAT represents hot emotion. Normally, there's no room in meetings to display emotion, so it ends up coloring our "logical" conclusions instead. What are we feeling about this issue? Excited? Afraid? Curious? Get it on the table.

BLACK HAT thinking is dark and cautious. This is where most of us excel—the Socratic thinking of Western civilization that reveres the "devil's advocate." Why is it likely that this new idea will fail? What are it's numerous weaknesses?

YELLOW HAT thinking is sunny and positive. Forget the devil's advocate for a moment. What greatness could come from this concept? Where can we see optimism and hope?

The GREEN HAT represents growth and creativity. What could we do that hasn't been done? How could some of our black hat fears be turned into opportunities?

The BLUE HAT is worn by the facilitator, who acts as referee and directs the use of the other hats. It represents cool objectivity.

By switching from hat to hat as the conversation requires, the group can quickly work through a huge number of ideas, unencumbered by flow-stopping arguments and emotion-laden attacks. The natural consequence of parallel thinking is large-scale buy-in, since the process is designed to be transparent and inclusive.

But how do you get the buy-in of those outside the original group? Hint: Not by blasting them with bullet points.

LEVER 8: BAN POWERPOINT

"Death by PowerPoint" is more than a wry phrase in most companies today. It's a full-blown epidemic. Tragically, the victims are company values such as collaboration, innovation, passion, vision, and clarity. Microsoft's presentation program is so ubiquitous that the word PowerPoint has become synonymous with copy-heavy slides—as in, "Can I drop a stack of PowerPoints on you?"

If you truly want buy-in, give PowerPoint a rest. Substitute more engaging techniques such as stories, demonstrations, drawings, prototypes, and brainstorming exercises. Admittedly, these may require skills that many executives have yet to perfect, but they're well worth mastering in the interest of a designful company.

Remember Richard Feynman's historic demonstration of how the rubber O-rings failed in the Challenger disaster? He riveted the audience's attention using a single O-ring, an ordinary clamp, and a glass of ice water. Of course, he could have picked his way through a deck of PowerPoint slides, reading bullet after point about safety factors, failure rates, resiliency ratios, and launch parameters, but somehow it wouldn't have created the same drama as simply unclamping the frozen O-ring to show that it was brittle.

This is not to say that slide presentations CAN'T be exciting. PowerPoints don't kill meetings, people do. There's very little about the software itself that dictates bad presentations. But there's very little that encourages GOOD presentations. The solution is to use presentation software in ways for which it was never intended—to communicate clearly, emotionally, and dramatically. Instead of using PowerPoint for convenience, use it the way Richard Feynman used his glass of ice water—to wake people up.

First, however, you'll have to renew your creative license. I'll quickly share three design rules we use at Neutron to turn slide shows into beacons of clarity.

1. EDIT TO THE BONE. Most slide presentations collapse under the weight of words. A good rule is ten per slide. This may seem strict, but limiting the number of words is the best way to make sure the ones you use will be read and understand. Ten words is about the maximum number that can fit on one line and still be read from the back row. If you need to use bullet points to make your case,

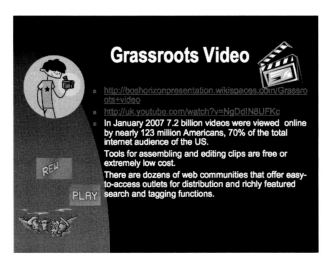

BEFORE

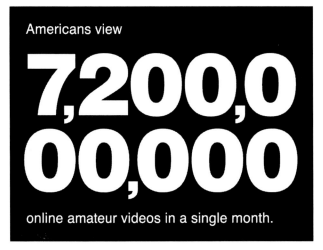

AFTER

create a "build"—adding one line of type at a time to keep your audience focused.

2. USE PICTURES. Even after editing, a steady diet of words is hard on the taste buds. Give your audience an occasional palette cleanser with illustrations, charts, diagrams, or photos. Whenever Lerner and Lowe felt that the dialogue in their musicals couldn't fully support the emotion of the story line, they inserted a song. Likewise, whenever you feel the text in your presentation can't fully support your key points, insert a picture.

3. KEEP IT MOVING. It's better to break slides into bite-sized ideas—usually one idea per slide—than to squeeze everything on one slide. Slides are free, so use them freely. It's preferable to see a hundred slides that move at a fast clip than be forced to stare a single slide for more than a minute.

If a business is really a decision factory, then the presentations that inform those decisions determine their quality. Decision-making is subject to the same law that governs software programming: garbage in, garbage out.

LEVER 9: SANCTION SPITBALLING

A common theme in business management is how to "empower employees." But wait a minute. Aren't employees hired to empower the company? What is the company, if not the employees?

If there's a conceptual error here, it lies in thinking there are two distinct classes of employees: those who come up with ideas, and those who implement them. Naturally, it's difficult to get employees excited about implementing initiatives they've had no hand in creating. You can empower like crazy and never generate enthusiasm among the disenfranchised class.

We've seen this happen in world governments as well. States that don't permit the free circulation of new ideas—especially ideas that are challenging or unflattering—are necessarily weak states. Economic expansion depends free expression, and governments that quash free expression inevitably lag behind those that encourage it.

The designful company, to a large extent, is a democratic company. While some organizational experts have suggested the company of the future will look like an "upside-down pyramid," a more apt description might be a "bottom-up pyramid."

Clearly, leaders must lead. But this doesn't mean they need to come up with all the ideas. In fact, you could argue that they needn't come up with ANY ideas, as long as good ideas are flowing up smoothly from the bottom. To make this happen, leaders will need to lighten the reins a bit. As Richard Teerlink said about his remarkable turn-around of Harley-Davidson, "You get power by releasing power."

FREE-SPEECH ZONES. The ability to speak freely should be an inalienable right in every company. Why? First of all, a broader dialogue yields better range of ideas. Second, when frustration is vented it can't build up pressure and explode inconveniently. And third, when cultural problems are spotted early on, they're much easier to fix. As one embittered employee said, writing anonymously on an unsanctioned blog, "You have to wonder about a CEO that needs a survey to find out if his employees are happy."

Instead of forcing employees to speak anonymously, why not encourage them to speak openly? Why not reward the messengers instead of shooting them? Facebook coo Sheryl Sandberg now asks her people to give frank feedback on whatever they see that is or isn't working. It's a lesson she learned early at Google before moving into the company's Facebook unit: "I thank every person who ever raised a problem publicly."

CONCEPT COLLECTION BOX. Google also uses an "idea management system" that allows employees to email innovative ideas for products, processes, and even businesses to a companywide suggestion box. Once ideas are collected, employees can then make comments on them and rate their chances for success. This type of open brainstorm is an inexpensive tool that any company can use to build a culture of innovation. Anyone in the company can sift through the resulting ideas to find one or more ideas worth developing further. Companies who adopt this technique will soon discover that good ideas don't care who they happen to.

THE 10% SOLUTION. Taking the collection box one step further, some companies are pushing employees to spend up to 10% of their time, or one day every two weeks, on the development of new ideas. Royal Dutch Shell, W.L. Gore, and Whirlpool are among the companies employing programs like these with notable success. Whirlpool expects their program to add more than $500 million a year to

A LEADER'S POWER INCREASES
IN DIRECT PROPORTION
TO THE UPWARD FLOW OF IDEAS.

the top line. Google, in true Google style, has raised the amount of elective time to 20% every employee.

GENIUS TEAMS. In addition to mining the wisdom of the crowd, companies can set up offline teams to crack any number of problems, whether routine or wicked. The advantage of this approach is that it moves a problem from the side of everyone's desk to the center, where it can command the maximum attention. Genius teams can contain anywhere from five to twenty members—a small enough number so that the effort to collaborate doesn't overwhelm the effort to solve the problem. To optimize the work of any team, small or large, you'll need a facilitator to act as referee, coach, and trainer. In some cases it pays to bring in an experienced facilitator from the outside.

Innovation is a numbers game. Winners are the companies that can increase the total number—if not the percentage—of viable options. Out of a 100 innovative ideas, only 15 may be worth prototyping and testing. Out of those 15, only five may be worth serious investment. Out of those five, one or two may produce game-changing results. It's a formula venture capitalists rely on, and one that established businesses would do well to adopt if they wish to compete at the speed of the market. When Steve Jobs was interviewed about how he intended to battle the Wintel monopoly, he replied: "I'm going to wait for the next big thing." Waiting, Steve Jobs-style, means bringing a large number of "insanely great" ideas to the brink of production, then focusing on the one or two most like to succeed at any given moment.

Yet even a talented CEO-designer like Jobs can't come up with all the ideas himself. Nor does he need to. All he needs to do is act as editor, subtracting the weak and superfluous ideas while augmenting the strong and essential ones. It helps, of course, that he can empathize with the desires of his customers, seeing not only the big picture but also able to zoom in on the details. He's well equipped to act as master facilitator of his creative metateam, pulling ideas up through the pyramid instead of driving them down from the top.

Revolution never starts at the top.

In ZAG I showed why companies repeatedly made the mistake of funding me-too projects—products, services, communications, businesses that have little hope of making a difference. To help decision-makers fight a natural tendency to overvalue the proven and undervalue the new, I proposed a tool called the "good/different chart," which groups new ideas into four patterns: 1) not good and not different; 2) good but not different; 3) good and different; 4) different but not good.

As you might guess, "good and different" is the combination that produces home runs. The Aeron chair, the Prius, Google search advertising, and Netflix are well-known examples of good and different. Yet companies are more likely to fund ideas that are either "good but not different" or "not good and not different." The reason is simple: New ideas are unpredictable, while existing ideas—no matter how weak—seem safe. What the good/different chart does is let decision-makers match a radical, unproven idea to a radical, proven idea from the past, thereby turning a leap of faith into a mere hop.

But how do you get a "good and different" idea past the hecklers and skeptics? It took 11 years for scientists Spencer Silver and Art Fry to run the concept of Post-it notes through he 3M product gantlet. Advertising genius George Lois had to threaten to jump from a 14-story window before the president of Levy's bread would signed off on one of the 1960s' iconic ad campaigns. Silicon Valley didn't take off until the so-called Traitorous Eight left the authoritarian Shockley lab to start their own company, Fairchild Semiconductor, in 1957.

These experiences suggest that great ideas can only succeed through acts of bravery. Maybe, but the design process can reduce the amount of bravery required. Designers are adept at moving ideas from impulse to hunch, hunch to sketch, sketch to prototype, and prototype to test, all without demanding risky financial commitments.

The biggest hurdle to innovation is the corporate longing for certainty about costs, market size, revenues, profits, and other quantities, all of which can't be known when an idea is new. Ironically, there seems to be no hurdle to investing in dying businesses, decaying strategies, and shrinking markets, all of which can be seen without a crystal ball. It seems we prefer the devil we know.

The best way to get around the devil—and all

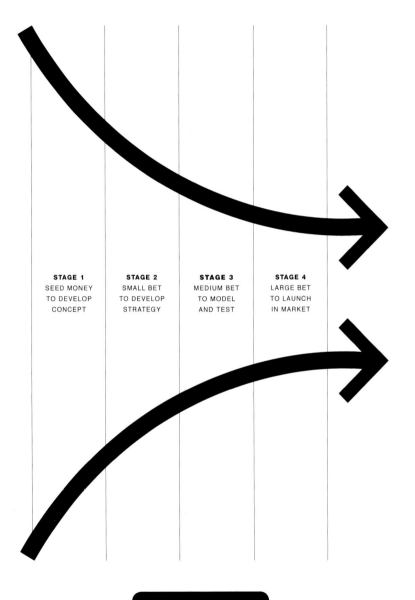

STAGE 1
SEED MONEY
TO DEVELOP
CONCEPT

STAGE 2
SMALL BET
TO DEVELOP
STRATEGY

STAGE 3
MEDIUM BET
TO MODEL
AND TEST

STAGE 4
LARGE BET
TO LAUNCH
IN MARKET

STAGE-GATE INNOVATION

his advocates—is to allow the company crank up its confidence stage by stage. Luckily, there's already a workable model for this process: stage-gate investing. It was pioneered by oil entrepreneurs who lacked certainty about which wells would produce black gold and which would fizzle. It was further developed by venture capitalists who lacked certainty about how ideas, markets, and business models would combine to produce profits.

There are four funding stages in this process: 1) seed money to develop the idea; 2) a small investment to design a strategy; 3) a medium investment to prototype and test it; and 4) a large investment to launch it into the market. With stage-gate investing, an idea is vetted stage by stage using a kind of natural selection, so that big bets are only made after the idea has been largely de-risked.

Stage-gate investing works best when you have a portfolio of innovations in the pipeline. The vetting process then acts a filtration system that separates the great ideas from those that are underpowered, short-sighted, unstrategic, or off-brand. The vetters themselves can be members of a specially selected innovation board, whose task it is to greenlight promising projects.

LEVER 11: DESIGN NEW METRICS

But how do you know if a project is promising, even WITH the stage-gate process? What formulas or measurements can you use to illuminate its chances at the next stage?

Here we enter one of the hottest debates in innovation: the value of metrics. It throws into sharp relief two seemingly opposed ways of thinking. The first is that decisions about new ideas should be based on evidence. The second is that new ideas can't be measured in advance. These two views are born of bitter experience. The experience of traditional business managers is that it's easy to be fooled by intuition, while the experience of traditional designers is that measurement can kill imagination. Yet what seems like a paradox actually hides a more interesting truth—that measurement and imagination are locked in a dance that they can either do badly or well.

The journey of the innovator, as one designer described it, is learning how to "cut cubes out of clouds." How can you give sharp edges to a soft concept so everyone can see it? How can you

IMAGINATION AND MEASUREMENT
ARE LOCKED IN A DANCE.

make the intangible tangible? It's folly to predict revenues, profits, costs, market share for product concept or business model that has yet to be introduced. But it's also folly to launch it without a modicum of analytical rigor. In the end, ALL innovations get measured—by the marketplace. The trick is to get a preview of those results before you commit the bulk of your resources.

Here are some measurements we've used at Neutron to empower both partners in the dance of innovation.

PRODUCT METRICS. In the early stages of product design, one-on-one customer interviews can be used to measure reactions to prototypes. They can answer questions about usability, desirability, understanding, cultural meaning, and emotional response, all of which can indicate potential success. They can also inspire new iterations and help you track your progress. As the project continues, you can monitor the number of customers contacted for input, the number of business partners lined up, the pace of development, and so on.

Across a whole portfolio of products, you can track quantities such as average time to market, number of pilot projects underway, and number and size of online communities. And you can gauge the general quality of your company's design from external sources such as blogs, professional reviews, and major award competitions. Don't scoff—The Design Council found that over a ten-year period the 61 top winners of the leading awards competitions outperformed the FTSE 100 by 200%.

COMMUNICATION METRICS. Here the aversion to being measured is actually measurable. In one study, over 90% of advertising creatives believed metrics to be "unhelpful," and nearly 65% believed them to be "harmful" to the creative process. My experience as a creative person suggests the reasons for this are two-fold: 1) most metrics are not aimed at enabling the creative process, and 2) creative people harbor a secret fear of losing their artistic freedom. Yet in reality, the testing of communication prototypes can be a creative person's best friend—it teaches valuable lessons about audience cognition, and frees creativity from the whimsical disapproval of uninformed decision-makers.

As with products, many types of communications—ads, packages, trademarks, and messages—can also be tested in quick one-on-one interviews with members of the target audience. They offer insights about the meaning of what you're presenting to people, allowing you to correct your course on the fly. And if you're serious about communicating, what's not to like?

Once communications are launched, you can measure outcomes such as audience awareness, comprehension, recall, and response. My preference, however, is to get a read on these levels BEFORE pressing the button.

BRAND METRICS. Since a brand is a commercial reputation, you can measure changes to the strength of that reputation year over year. You can also measure the asset value of a brand, as well as the brand's influence on purchase decisions. You can monitor the number of brand-loyal versus non-brand-loyal customers, and measure their understanding and their recall of brand elements.

If your company is one of the top 100 brands, you can get a free valuation simply by looking it up on Interbrand's Best Global Brands. If not, you can commission your own valuation. The main thing is to be consistent, using the same formula to measure your brand from year to year.

PILOT PROJECTS UNDERWAY
PACE OF PRODUCT DEVELOPMENT
USABILITY OF PROTOTYPES
DESIRABILITY OF PROTOTYPES
DIFFERENTIATION FROM COMPETITORS
LEVEL OF USER EXCITEMENT
CULTURAL MEANING OF CONCEPT
INTENT TO PURCHASE
RANKING AGAINST COMPETING CHOICES
POTENTIAL PRICE ELASTICITY
NUMBER OF CUSTOMERS CONTACTED
NUMBER OF PARTNERS CONTACTED
AVERAGE TIME TO MARKET
LEVEL OF SPENDING ON DESIGN
COST SAVINGS FROM DESIGN
EXCESS RENTS FROM DESIGN
NUMBER OF EXTERNAL DESIGN AWARDS
READABILITY OF MESSAGING
COMPREHENSION OF ELEMENTS
RECALL OF ELEMENTS
NUMBER OF LEADS GENERATED
ADVERTISEMENTS SEEN AND NOTED
PACKAGING SHELF IMPACT
PERCENTAGE OF EMAILS OPENED
PERCENTAGE OF CLICK-THROUGHS
NUMBER OF HITS TO LANDING PAGE
COMPLETED ONLINE FORMS
NUMBER OF BLOG MENTIONS
STRENGTH OF ONLINE COMMENTS
SHARE OF MIND VS. COMPETITION
LEVEL OF BRAND AWARENESS
LEVEL OF BRAND RECOGNITION
TOTAL BRAND VALUATION
STRENGTH OF CUSTOMER LOYALTY
GROWTH OF CUSTOMER COMMUNITY
BRAND DIFFERENTIATION
UNIQUENESS OF BRAND ASSOCIATIONS
BRAND PREFERENCES
WILLINGNESS TO RECOMMEND
COMPETITIVE RANKING
INFLUENCE ON PURCHASE
LEVEL OF EMOTION CREATED
NUMBER OF REPEAT PURCHASES
MARKET PENETRATION
LEVEL OF CUSTOMER SATISFACTION
AVERAGE RETENTION COST
GROWTH OF CUSTOMER COMMUNITIES
LEVEL OF EMPLOYEE ENGAGEMENT
NUMBER OF BRAND-TRAINED EMPLOYEES
NUMBER OF INTERNAL DESIGNERS
EMPLOYEE SATISFACTION
UNDERSTANDING OF MISSION AND VISION
EMPLOYEE CONTRIBUTION TO BRAND
NUMBER OF COLLABORATORS
NUMBER OF NEW IDEAS SUBMITTED
PROFITS PER EMPLOYEE
RETURN ON OVERALL DESIGN INVESTMENT
SAVINGS FROM PROCESS IMPROVEMENT
WEALTH CREATION WITHIN DOMAIN

THINGS THAT CAN BE MEASURED

CULTURE METRICS. For many corporate managers, culture is a cloudy concept. So if you're about to embark on a culture-change program, it pays to measure your progress every step of the way, from the original state to the desired state. This is not as difficult as it seems, since a lot of the work can be done with internal polls. In the case of a demoralized workforce, the act of polling itself can restart the flow of hope.

A culture change can begin by measuring the existing level of employee satisfaction. A neglected culture will often start out with very low scores, but the level will climb quickly as you apply the levers of transformation. As each lever is applied, there are multiple opportunities to measure the results.

Now, a caveat.

As handy as metrics are for de-risking innovation, they have their limitations. As Dr. Deming said, "The most important things cannot be measured." In other words, measurability decreases as importance increases. Our penchant for metrics comes from the resounding success of industrial-age finance. Yet there are no generally accepted accounting principles for new ideas. The yardstick has not been invented that can measure the precise long-term potential of a breakthrough brand.

In an era when financial performance comes more and more from intangible assets, we'll need to invent sophisticated metrics to predict the value of innovation, and nuanced accounting principles to measure the return on creativity. Of course, truly innovative ideas shouldn't need much help from metrics. If an opportunity is off the charts, there's no point in saying it's two times off the charts. Just make sure it's good enough and different enough to sustain a business, then design it forward to see where it goes.

LEVER 12: INSTITUTE BRANDED TRAINING

Creative work can't be Taylorized. It can't be reduced to a series of steps or run through a production line. No two creative solutions are alike, and no two creative people are alike. The best you can do is build a shared understanding of the principles of design so that everyone in the company has a chance to experiment, to learn, and to grow as a group.

In an age of accelerating change, HOW you learn is vastly more important than WHAT you learn. The ability to acquire new knowledge quickly is the fundamental skill that underpins a culture of innovation. "Every enterprise is a learning and teaching institution," said Drucker. "Training and development must be built into it at all levels— training and development that never stop." If you want a culture of non-stop innovation, you need a system of non-stop training.

What kind of training?

Training that bridges the gap between university knowledge and industry knowledge, and between industry knowledge and company knowledge.

Training that teaches personal mastery, and training that teaches collaboration, so that personal mastery can inform collaboration and vice versa.

Training that explores how employees can build the value of the brand, how they can help create customer delight, and how they can align their individual actions with overall business strategy.

This is known as branded training. It's a type of education custom-fitted to the company's brand, culture, and mission. Without branded training, one company's skills and knowledge would look much like another's, and no company would gain a competitive advantage. If this is the situation in your industry, you have an unparalleled opportunity to steal a march on your competitors. If, on the other hand, your competitors are already using branded training, you can't afford to let this threat to go unchallenged. First they'll woo your customers. Next they'll woo your employees.

Paychex is a national accounting service that uses training to build their brand and raise the bar against competition. They lavish an average of 107 hours of training on each employee. The company recently won a strong recommendation in FORTUNE's "100 Best Companies to Work for."

ICES

OF THE
MEETING

BRANDS WITH
NEW MEDIA

OF THE
MEETING

GING
ND
OLS

HOW TO LEAD
CREATIVE PEOPLE

THE ART
OF CUSTOMER
DELIGHT

MASTERING
THE CREATIVE
PROCESS

PING
STOMER
NEY

A BRANDED
TRANING PROGRAM
CAN JUMPSTART
A CULTURE
OF INNOVATION

QUICK-TESTING
CREATIVE
SOLUTIONS

EVALUATING
INNOVATIVE
CONCEPTS

E ART
THE
TING

HOW TO LIVE
THE BRAND

HARNESSING
COMMUNITIES
OF INTEREST

HOW TO
DIFFERENTIATE
BY DESIGN

RSHIP
ND
WSHIP

POSITIONING
FOR COMPETITIVE
ADVANTAGE

TELLING THE
CORPORATE STORY

SECRETS
OF MARKET
RESEARCH

EGIES
EATIVE
WORK

THE ART OF
POWERFUL
PRESENTATIONS

MANAGING
BRAND
EXTENSIONS

BUILDING
A CREATIVE
METATEAM

NAME

THE FINE ART

HOW TO BUILD

THE FINE ART

The Four Seasons Hotels and Resorts has invested heavily in training and recruitment to "make people feel great." Now that the organization has raised it's service to the first-class level, where do you think the young talent wants to work?

Whirlpool has made innovation a top priority. The company has trained more than 600 innovation mentors, and enrolled every employee in an online innovation course. Now every product development plan at Whirlpool contains new-to-market innovations.

In the 1990s, Samsung used branded training to lift itself from a me-too manufacturer to a maker of high-design products. Chairman Kun-Hee Lee backed up his demand for a more designful culture by building a $10 million, eight-story building in Korea to house Samsung's Innovation Design Lab. For a full year, employees were paid their normal salaries to study there six days a week. The company soon increased its stake with more labs in San Francisco, Los Angeles, London, Tokyo, and China.

Today, Samsung has built a vibrant culture of innovation that includes 380 company-trained designers helping to launch 100 products per year. They've earned 18 major industrial design awards over the last five years, and five awards from

BusinessWeek/IDSA alone, a total matched only by Apple Computer. Two years in a row, Interbrand's annual brand survey declared Samsung the world's "fastest growing brand."

While large companies like Samsung can build their own learning programs, small companies and departmental teams can avail themselves of external courses and workshops, many of which can be customized for the company.

"Intellectual assets will determine a company's value in the 21st century," said VP of design Kook Hyun Chung. "The age when companies simply sell products is over." Today, winning companies are those that can respond to emerging opportunities and unmet customer needs at the speed of the market. There is no practical way to develop that ability without learning—as a collaborative community—new ways to be creative.

LEVER 13: LEARN THROUGH ACQUISITION

A common observation of mergers and acquisitions is that they often fail, or at least fail to deliver on the full promise of synergy. Among the reasons given for bad M&A experiences are conflicting capabilities, cultural differences, operational distraction, and the inability to resolve identity issues. What gets lost in the analysis is the emotional resistance felt by the acquired or smaller company. The traditional impulse of the to force it into an unfamiliar mold, which is exceedingly painful and unproductive.

In reality, it's impossible to force one culture to conform to another. You can't put braces on people's brains, nor corrective shoes on their behaviors. If you try, what you get is an underground battle of wills that harms both sides of the acquisition and delays the benefits of synergy.

The solution? Reverse the impulse. Instead of viewing the acquired company as an uneducated child, view it as an inspired teacher. Smaller companies are usually acquired as a result of deep-domain knowledge, special focus, or extreme passion. By mining the acquired company for a better understanding of its success factors, both cultures gain and the marriage can more quickly succeed.

LEVER 14: ADD A SEAT TO THE TABLE

Whether companies are acquisitive or not, as they grow they tend to put up organizational walls that inhibit collaboration and knowledge sharing. The quickest way to reconnect the silos is to encourage representatives from each silo meet regularly to raise cultural issues and explore opportunities for cross-fertilization and creative collaboration. This committee, whether it's called an innovation council, brand committee, or design board, should be led by an executive at the top of the company. This is not a part-time or temporary assignment. It can't be managed from the side of the CMO's desk or jobbed out to a consulting firm.

The simplest approach is to place a Chief Brand Officer in this role. The CBO's task is to shepherd the growth and value of the corporate brand, including all its feeders—subbrands, identity systems, design inputs, innovation processes, advertising programs, communications, training— so that the whole is more than the sum of its parts. Depending on the strategic needs of the company, the actual title may vary—Chief Design Officer, Chief Innovation Officer, VP of Creativity, or any label that signals a serious commitment to design.

There's only one problem: Where do you find a person who has both the strategic and creative chops to integrate the design of everything the company makes, says, and does? So far there are no university programs that graduate students with degrees in Innovation Administration. There are, however, a growing list of programs that combine business and design (IIT), art and engineering (Stanford), design and strategy (CCA), and brand and business (Kellogg).

Yet until graduates of these programs have proven themselves in the crucible of the market-place, it's best to fill this position from a pool of executives whose talents have led them on a tour of relevant, real-world experiences.

For example, Amy Curtis-McIntyre gained experience in various marketing, advertising, and communications jobs before heading up brand communications at JetBlue and later Hyatt Hotels. Claudia Kotchka held jobs in accounting, marketing, and management before rising to chief of design innovation at P&G. Sam Lucente was an industrial designer at IBM, the director of user experience at Netscape, and founder of his own firm before being tapped as vice president of design at HP.

INNOVATION
FLOURISHES BEST
WHEN DESIGN HAS
A SEAT AT THE TABLE.

LEVER 15: RECOGNIZE TALENT

As we move from the spreadsheet era to the creative era, economic value will come from human networks more than electronic ones. Companies will create wealth from the conversion of raw intangibles—imagination, empathy, and collaboration—into finished intangibles—patents, brands, and customer tribes. Economic value will be measured less in terms of return on capital than return on creativity. So how do you measure talent? How do you increase inspiration? How do you crank up creative joy?

The answer to all of these is the same: recognition. While the spreadsheet era was focused on perfection, the creative era is focused on excellence. And there's no quicker way to get the flywheel of innovation spinning at high speed than to reward excellence through a high-profile recognition program.

Here's the formula. Start with a clear articulation of the company's goals (lever 3), so that you have the right criteria for judging the work.

Then define the categories in a way that places emphasis where you want it (for example, best product design, best sales event, best new

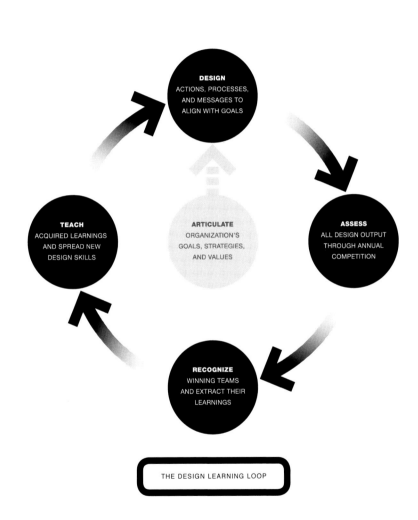

THE DESIGN LEARNING LOOP

process, best integrated program). Line up respected experts from inside and outside the company to judge the entries. Let the entrants know that the winners will be chosen not only for alignment with the company's goals, but for the measurable outcomes of their individual projects (lever 11).

Next, celebrate the winning entries with an event. It can be as small as a modest dinner, or as large as a three-day conference.

Of course, you could stop right there. But you'd be wasting a priceless chance to turn recognition into education. What if you edited the comments of the external judges into lively video critiques? Published reviews of the entries on the online innovation center? Shared the learnings from this year's output, so that next year's output could stand on its shoulders? Even used the learnings, reviews, and critiques to build out a series of training modules? Then you'd have a perpetual-motion machine for driving higher and higher levels of design, and for spreading a culture of innovation into every corner of the enterprise.

LEVER 16: REWARD WITH WICKED PROBLEMS

While most employees appreciate public acclaim and the occasional monetary award, the highest achievers want something more. They want bigger problems. They want an opportunity to tackle mean, hairy challenges and make a significant contribution to the company.

In THE SUPPORT ECONOMY, authors Zuboff and Maxmin observe that companies haven't keep pace with the culture at large, because people no longer want jobs—they want support to fulfill their dreams. IBM is a company that gets it. The company recognizes outstanding research scientists by bestowing on them the lifetime status of "IBM Scientist." Along with this title comes several years of time and seed money to develop leading-edge science and technology for the company.

This is one reason why Google has been rated the number-one company to work for. Far from discouraging risk-taking, the company actually demands it. You can't "organize the world's information and make it universally accessible and useful" without overcoming a few obstacles.

What wicked problems exist at your company? How can you turn hairy obstacles into high-status rewards? Who out there looks hungry for a challenge?

A SUFFICIENTLY ADVANCED CULTURE.

The late science-fiction author Arthur C. Clarke remarked that "any sufficiently advanced technology is indistinguishable from magic." The same could be said about designful companies. As we transition from the spreadsheet era to the creative era, design thinking will undoubtedly prove elusive to some, problematic to others, and baffling to others. Months ago, while I explained the thesis of my book to my friend Paul, a talented accountant, he listened with furrowed brow. "It sounds logical," he finally said, "but I'm having trouble imagining how it would FEEL to work in a company like that." Fair enough. So before I let you go, I'll try to summarize the emotional benefits of working in a designful company.

In a traditional company, the focus is on costs, while in the designful company it's on customers. This puts a premium on the ability to empathize with people outside the company, which creates a feeling of connectedness.

In a traditional company, the dominant mode is command and control, while in a designful company it's vision and creativity. The corresponding feelings are excitement and satisfaction.

In a traditional company, jobs are role-oriented, while in a designful company they're project-oriented. As a result, respect comes from merit more than position, which imparts a feeling of self-esteem.

In a traditional company, risk-taking is discouraged, while in a designful company it's part of the innovation process. Therefore a can-do feeling replaces a can't-do feeling.

In a traditional company, workers are siloed, while in a designful company they collaborate. This creates a feeling of shared success.

In a traditional company, beauty is tacked on, while in a designful company it's built in. It's part of the way products are made, the way people are treated, and the way decisions are designed. The feeling we get from caring about beauty is hope for the future.

In an age of wicked problems, companies can no longer simply "unlock" wealth. Today they must actively "create" wealth to keep up with the speed of change. For the first time since the Industrial Revolution, successful companies will be designful companies. They'll combine knowing, making, and doing to strive for truth, beauty, and the public good. At last, the bottom line will begin to trace the shape of who we want to be.

CHANGE IS POWER.

DESIGN IS CHANGE.

TAKE-HOME LESSONS

If you don't have time to read the entire text, or if you'd like a recap, here's a quick summary of the ideas covered in THE DESIGNFUL COMPANY. Sprinkle liberally throughout your presentations, or try adding a different one to the bottom of each business e-mail you send—you may be surprised at the conversations you'll start.

WICKED PROBLEMS

→ We've been getting better and better at a management model that's getting wronger and wronger.

→ The new management model must replace the win-lose nature of the assembly line with the win-win nature of the network.

→ The management innovation that's destined to kick Six Sigma off its throne is design thinking. It will take over your marketing department, move into you R&D labs, transform your processes, and ignite your culture.

→ If you wanna innovate, you gotta design.

→ Design is rapidly spreading from "posters and toasters" to processes, systems, and organizations.

→ Design drives innovation; innovation powers brand; brand builds loyalty; and loyalty sustains profits. If you want long-term profits, start with design.

→ There are really only two main components for business success: brands and their delivery.

→ The central problem of brand-building is getting a complex organization to execute a simple idea.

→ Difference plus design equals delight.

→ Agility is an emergent property that appears when an organization has the right mindset, the right skills, and the ability to multiply those skills through collaboration.

→ It's one thing to inject a company WITH inventiveness. It's another thing to build a company ON inventiveness.

→ The problem with consumerism isn't that it creates desire, but that it fails to fully satisfy it. Part of what we desire is to feel good about the things we buy.

→ People have more buying choices, so they're choosing in favor of beauty, simplicity, and the "tribal identity" of their favorite brands.

THE POWER OF DESIGNING

→ For businesses to bottle the kind of experiences that focus minds and intoxicate hearts, they'll need to do more than HIRE designers. They'll need to BE designers.

→ A designer is anyone who tries to change an existing situation to an improved one.

→ The best design thinkers tend to be empathetic, intuitive, imaginative, and idealistic.

→ The gap between "what is" and "what could be" is filled with creative tension—a powerful source of energy for creative people.

→ Imagine a capitalist society running entirely on "what is" thinking: Nothing would be ventured and nothing gained.

→ The traditional management model is a veritable thrift store of hand-me-down concepts, all designed for a previous need and a previous era.

→ You can't DECIDE the way forward. You have to DESIGN the way forward.

→ When the left brain and right brain work together, a third brain emerges that can do what neither brain can do alone.

→ Third-brain thinkers don't settle for easy options— they work until they find the win-win ground among seemingly opposing sets of needs.

→ Designful leaders reject the tyranny of "or" in favor of the genius of "and".

→ The designful leader and the creative artist are one in the same.

→ Rule-busting innovation requires a sense of play—a refusal to be corralled by a strict method.

→ Industrial Age companies emphasized two main activities: knowing and doing. The designful company inserts a third activity: making.

→ Designers use non-logical processes that are difficult to express in words but easier to express in action.

→ In the making mode, designers learn what they're doing while they're doing it.

→ The most innovative designers consciously reject the standard option box and cultivate an appetite for "thinking wrong."

→ Many times thinking wrong is just wrong, but sometimes it turns out more right than right.

→ If you want to drive your stock price higher— and sustain it—you need to first invest in vision, culture, and innovation.

→ In a company with an innovative culture, radical
  ideas are the norm, not the exception.

→ The higher design moves up the ladder, the
  more leverage it delivers.

→ Aesthetics gives us a toolbox for beautiful execution.

→ There are shapes, sounds, scents, juxtapositions,
  and patterns that push our emotional buttons
  no matter who we are, where we live, or what
  we believe in.

→ The more technological our culture becomes,
  the more we need the sensual and metaphorical
  power of beauty.

→ We ascribe beauty to the things we admire,
  then we begin to admire things that exhibit the
  same beauty.

→ We often use beauty as a proxy for quality.

→ Since aesthetics is reinforced by simplicity and efficiency, it offers a powerful tool for thriving in an era of diminishing natural resources.

→ Good design does not depend so much on the eye of the beholder, but on a combination of aesthetics and ethics. Good design exhibits virtues.

→ For the first time since the Industrial Age, successful businesses will be designful businesses.

LEVERS FOR CHANGE

→ With the efficiency of a flywheel, a culture of innovation builds momentum with very small inputs, but can release large amounts of stored energy when needed.

→ Companies don't fail because they choose the wrong course—they fail because they can't imagine a better one.

→ While revolution must be led from the top, it rarely starts at the top.

→ Stories rise uncontrollably from our desire to explain and share human experience. They can be powerful building blocks for culture.

→ The Information Age has been hailed as the successor to the Industrial Age. But the true gift of digital invention is not information but collaboration.

→ Before you can build an internal design capability, you need to address the problem of "vanishing respect."

→ If the future of corporate design depends on the metateam, then the critical role of the internal design department is to manage it.

→ Like brand management, design management should NEVER be outsourced. Conversely, many of the design skills needed to execute brand-related projects should ALWAYS be outsourced.

→ Strong-willed people love to collaborate when there's a sharp delineation of roles, an unobstructed view of the goal, and a strong commitment to quality.

→ Creativity can be exercised in two modes: team creativity and individual creativity. The key is finding a collaborative rhythm that incorporates both modes.

→ PowerPoint has become a full-blown epidemic. Tragically, the victims are company values such as collaboration, innovation, passion, vision, and clarity.

→ If you want buy-in, give PowerPoint a rest. Substitute more engaging techniques such as stories, demonstrations, drawings, prototypes, and brainstorming exercises.

→ If a business is a decision factory, then the presentations that inform those decisions determine their quality: garbage in, garbage out.

→ Leaders must lead. But this doesn't mean they need to come up with all the ideas. In fact, you could argue that they needn't come up with ANY ideas, as long as good ideas are flowing up smoothly from the bottom.

→ Innovation is a numbers game. Winners are the companies that can increase the total number—if not the percentage—of viable options.

→ The biggest hurdle to innovation is the corporate longing for certainty about costs, market size, revenues, profits, and other quantities, all of which can't be known when an idea is new.

→ Ironically, there seems to be no hurdle to investing in dying businesses, decaying strategies, and shrinking markets, all of which can be seen without a crystal ball.

→ With stage-gate investing, an idea is vetted stage by stage using a kind of natural selection, so that big bets are only made after the idea has been largely de-risked.

→ The journey of the innovator is learning how to "cut cubes out of clouds."

→ In the end, ᴀʟʟ innovations get measured—by the marketplace. The trick is to get a preview of those results before you commit the bulk of your resources.

→ If you're about to embark on a culture-change program, it pays to measure your progress every step of the way, from the original state to the desired state.

→ A neglected culture will often start out with very low scores, but the level will climb quickly as you apply the levers of transformation.

→ As handy as metrics are for de-risking innovation, they have their limitations. Measurability decreases as importance increases.

→ Truly innovative ideas don't need much help from metrics. If an opportunity is off the charts, there's no point in saying it's two times off the charts.

→ In an age of accelerating change, HOW you learn is vastly more important than WHAT you learn. The ability to acquire new knowledge quickly is the fundamental skill that underpins a culture of innovation.

→ Without branded training, one company's skills and knowledge would look much like another's, and no company would gain a competitive advantage.

→ It's impossible to force one culture to conform to another. You can't put braces on people's brains, nor corrective shoes on their behaviors.

→ Instead of viewing an acquired company as an uneducated child, view it as an inspired teacher.

→ As we move from the spreadsheet era to the creative era, economic value will come from human networks more than electronic ones.

→ Successful companies will create wealth from the conversion of raw intangibles—imagination, empathy, and collaboration—into finished intangibles—patents, brands, and customer tribes.

→ How do you measure talent? How do you increase inspiration? How do you crank up creative joy? The answer to all of these is the same: recognition.

→ A recognition program creates a perpetual-motion machine for driving higher and higher levels of design and spreading a culture of "innovation into every corner of the enterprise.

→ While most employees appreciate public acclaim and the occasional monetary award, the highest achievers want something more. They want wicked problems.

Remember the top-ten wicked problems from page 2? Here's how design can begin to solve them.

WICKED PROBLEMS	WICKED SOLUTIONS
1. BALANCING LONG-TERM SUCCESS WITH SHORT-TERM DEMANDS	Articulate a long-term vision Build a culture of innovation Strive for charismatic brands Encourage organic customer loyalty Institute branded training Give design a seat at the table
2. PREDICTING THE RETURNS ON INNOVATIVE CONCEPTS	Screen for "good and different" Use designing instead of deciding Bring design management inside Think big, spend small Use stage-gate innovation Design new metrics
3. INNOVATING AT THE INCREASING SPEED OF CHANGE	Build a culture of innovation Focus on agility instead of ownership move Move design up the ladder Let ideas flow upward Institute branded training Reward with wicked problems
4. WINNING THE WAR FOR FIRST-CLASS TALENT	Paint a bold picture of the future Tackle wicked problems Weave a rich story Knock down the walls Institute branded training Recognize talent
5. COMBINING PROFITABILITY AND SOCIAL RESPONSIBILITY	Use designing instead of deciding Apply aesthetics to management Strive for "good design" Treat responsibility as a design opportunity Institute branded training Reward good brand behavior

WICKED PROBLEMS	WICKED SOLUTIONS
6. PROTECTING MARGINS IN A COMMODITIZING INDUSTRY	Strive for charismatic brands Encourage organic customer loyalty Build a culture of innovation Bring design management inside, Institute branded training Recognize talent
7. MULTIPLYING SUCCESS BY COLLABORATING ACROSS SILOS	Assemble a metateam Bring design management inside Establish an innovation center Institute branded training Recognize talent Give design a seat at the table
8. FINDING UNCLAIMED YET PROFITABLE MARKETSPACE	Screen for "good and different" Use designing instead of deciding Build a culture of innovation Let ideas flow upward Use stage-gate innovation Design new metrics
9. ADDRESSING THE CHALLENGE OF ECO-SUSTAINABILITY	Tackle wicked problems Design for efficiency Take design cues from nature, Strive for "good design" Let ideas flow upward Use stage-gate innovation
10. ALIGNING STRATEGY WITH CUSTOMER EXPERIENCE	Bring design management inside Assemble a creative metateam Collaborate concertina-style Let ideas flow upward Institute branded training Give design a seat at the table

RECOMMENDED READING

CLOSING THE INNOVATION GAP, Judy Estrin (McGraw-Hill, 2008). With mounting problems facing business, education, and the government, entrepreneur Estrin says our ability to innovate has been seriously compromised. She makes a passionate plea for reigniting global creativity through a sustainable "ecosystem" of innovation. What's missing, she says, is the robust interplay of research, development, and application. Includes scores of interviews with innovation leaders.

DESIGN MANAGEMENT, Brigitte Borja de Mozota (Alworth Press, 2003). French researcher de Mozota collected case studies from 37 companies—including BMW, Braun, Nike, Sony, Dyson, and others—to illuminate the growing interest in design management as a core business activity. A design manager by experience, de Mozota extracts a number of best practices from these studies and presents a range of methodologies for turning talent into value.

THE FUTURE OF MANAGEMENT, Gary Hamel (Harvard Business School Press, 2007). Business professor Hamel brings considerable credibility to the topic of modern management. Here he says that the world is ready for the next big management innovation, and to achieve it we must throw off the chains of traditional thinking. He marshals a number of examples from innovative companies such as Google and W.L. Gore (the makers of Gore-Tex) to illustrate his provocative points.

INNOVATION AND ENTREPRENEURSHIP, Peter Drucker (Harper & Row, 1985). This is the first book to present innovation as systematic discipline worthy of management focus. Drucker believed that entrepreneurship is not only possible in all organizations, but necessary for their survival. His book was right on time for the digital revolution, and, like all of Drucker's books, has aged gracefully.

LEADING THE REVOLUTION, Gary Hamel (Plume, 2000). Hamel issues a call to arms for would-be revolutionaries, saying it's not enough to develop one or two innovative products—in the 21st century you need to create a state of perpetual innovation, not just with products but whole business models. Once an innovation becomes a best practice, he says, it's potency is lost. "If it's not different, it's not strategic." Highly recommended for provocateurs at every rung of the corporate ladder.

MOBILIZING MINDS, Lowell Bryan and Claudia Joyce (McGraw-Hill, 2007). If you're the kind of person who needs concrete formulas instead of principles, this book is for you. But if you want your formulas to be market-tested, you may still be insecure about implementing these ideas. They include a radical flattening of organizational structure, front-line managers who are free to make tactical decisions, a one-company governance and culture, and talent marketplaces. Personally, I find these ideas refreshing and well suited to a designful company.

OUT OF THE CRISIS, W. Edwards Deming (The MIT Press, 2000). Originally published in 1982, this was Dr. Deming's recipe for business transformation, based on his famous 14 Points for Management. He believed that leadership should be judged not only by the quarterly dividend, but by innovative plans to stay in business. Some of his directives: Replace short-term reaction with long-term planning, drive out fear so people can work, and break down barriers between departments.

REVOLUTIONARY WEALTH, Alvin and Heidi Toffler (Knopf, 2006). No one who tries to peak at the future can afford to ignore the Tofflers. Their earlier books, **FUTURE SHOCK**, **THE THIRD WAVE**, and **POWERSHIFT**, were the tea leaves of the digital generation. Here they show that Industrial Age economics are inadequate for understanding 21st-century money. "Prosuming," they say, will soon compel radical changes in the way we measure, make, and manipulate wealth.

CREATIVE THINKING   **HARE BRAIN, TORTOISE MIND**, Guy Claxton (The Ecco Press, 1999). Most business people prefer making quick decisions to "sleeping on it." New research suggests that patience and confusion—rather than rigor and certainty—are the essential components of wisdom. Claxton encourages a reevaluation of results-oriented problem solving, preferring the slower intuition of the "tortoise mind" to the facile speed of the "hare brain."

HOW THE MIND WORKS, Steven Pinker (W. W. Norton & Company, 1999). Pinker is the leading popular writer on the brain and cognitive psychology. In this book he argues that the theories of computational processing and natural selection have conspired to give us good vision, group living, free hands, and superior hunting skills. These in turn have led us to an appreciation for art, music, literature, and philosophy. This big, heavy book is made lighter by Pinker's welcome sense of humor.

MANAGING AS DESIGNING, Richard Boland and Fred Collopy (Stanford Business Books, 2004). Drawing from their personal experience as clients of Frank Gehry, business professors Boland and Collopy explore the difference between the "decision attitude" and the "design attitude." Their thesis is that decisions are more powerful when they're "designed."

THE OPPOSABLE MIND, Roger Martin (Harvard Business School Press, 2007). Martin is the dean of the Rotman School of Management, and a strong proponent of design thinking in business strategy. The opposable mind, analogous to the opposable thumb, allows leaders to grasp and resolve the tensions inherent in difficult problems, using a model called "integrative thinking." He also suggests that "mastery without originality becomes rote," as well as the converse, "originality without mastery is flaky if not entirely random."

THE RISE OF THE CREATIVE CLASS, Richard Florida (Basic Books, 2003). Florida is a social planner who asserts that the creative class—38 million people including scientists, engineers, architects, educators, writers, artists, and entertainers—is profoundly influencing the future of the work-place. He calls for the creative class to claim its place in society and take responsibility for improving the common good.

THE SCIENCES OF THE ARTIFICIAL, Herbert Simon (The MIT Press,1996). Though the first edition appeared 40 years ago, Simon's ideas remain remarkably fresh and provocative today. Here he continues his exploration into the organization of complexity and the science of design. He takes on themes such as chaos, adaptive systems, and genetic algorithms to better understand the nature of complex systems. A somewhat difficult but rewarding read for those interested in design thinking and artificial intelligence.

A WHOLE NEW MIND, Daniel Pink (Riverhead Trade, 2006). Pink claims that the key to success in the future is cultivating six right-brain senses: design, story, symphony, empathy, play, and meaning. Jobs that don't require these traits will be outsourced or automated. Two memorable quotes from Pink: "The MFA is the new MBA," and "Meaning is the new money."

THE BRAND GAP, Marty Neumeier (New Riders/AIGA, 2003). This, the first of my whiteboard overviews, shows companies how to bridge the gap between business strategy and customer experience. It defines brand-building as a system that includes five disciplines: differentiation, collaboration, innovation, validation, and cultivation. Like my second book, **ZAG**, it's designed as an "airplane book"—a two-hour read that can also serve as a reference tool. Look for the second edition, which includes all the definitions from **THE DICTIONARY OF BRAND**.

DESIGNING BRAND IDENTITY, Alina Wheeler (John Wiley & Sons, 2006). A brand isn't truly differentiated until its personality is made visible through its touchpoints. Wheeler's book presents winning examples of trademarks and other graphic communications, and offers a cogent description of how strategy and creativity meet in the real world among world-class companies. An indispensable reference tool that sets the bar where it should be—extremely high. Look for the updated third edition.

THE DICTIONARY OF BRAND, edited by Marty Neumeier (AIGA, 2004). This pocket-sized book is only available through Amazon. Published by AIGA, the professional association for design, it's the first book to "regularize" common brand terms. To get agreement on the definitions, I assembled an advisory council of ten thought leaders from the fields of management, advertising, market research, business publishing, and design. You can also get the definitions in **THE BRAND GAP** expanded edition.

ZAG, Marty Neumeier (New Riders/AIGA, 2007). Whereas **THE BRAND GAP** outlined the five disciplines needed to build a charismatic brand, **ZAG** drills down into the first of the disciplines, radical differentiation. In an age of me-too products and instant communications, winning companies are those that can out-position, out-maneuver, and out-design the competition. The rule? When everybody zigs, zag.

ECO-DESIGN   **BIOMIMICRY**, Janine Benyus (Harper Perennial, 2002). Nature is the greatest designer, an apt model for a new industrial ecology. Benyus hints at the great potential profitability of copying some of nature's time-tested inventions. She proposed ten lessons that an ecologically aware company, culture, or economy could draw on to promote a healthier, more sustainable, and even more affluent future.

CRADLE TO CRADLE, William McDonough and Michael Braungart (North Point Press, 2002). What if products could be designed so that at the end of their useful lives they could provide nourishment for something new? Or what if they could provide "technical nutrients" that would re-circulate in closed-loop industrial cycles? Architect McDonough and chemist Braungart show that "cradle to grave" manufacturing is not only wasteful but unnecessary in light of recent scientific discoveries. A seminal work on the topic.

DESIGN AND THE ELASTIC MIND, Hugh Aldersey-Williams et al (The Museum of Modern Art, 2008). This brain-bending volume is the book version an influential museum exhibition curated by Paola Antonelli for MoMA in New York. It demonstrates how designers are able to transform recent advances in technology into wondrous objects, systems, and possible futures. Get ready to be amazed.

THE ECOLOGY OF COMMERCE, Paul Hawkin (Collins, 1994). The man behind the Smith & Hawkin garden tool empire is no traditional capitalist. In his continuing crusade to transform our economic system, he proposes that we stop accelerating the rate at which we draw down capacity, refrain from degrading other people's environments, and avoid displacing other species by taking over their habitats. Wall Street may not have been ready for his message in 1994, but it's listening now.

AESTHETICS

FROM LASCAUX TO BROOKLYN, Paul Rand (Yale University Press, 1996). Rand, graphic design's most erudite practitioners, published a passionate plea for better aesthetics just before he died in 1996. Here he shows why the cave paintings at Lascaux—and other timeless works of art—have universal qualities that transcend era, place, purpose, style, or genre. He then uses examples from his own work to show how designers can incorporate them into the modern world.

THE LAWS OF SIMPLICITY, John Maeda (The MIT Press, 2006). Noted designer and MIT professor Maeda offers ten laws for balancing simplicity and complexity to improve business, technology, and design. He demonstrates how our notion of "more is better" is undermining the quality of customer experiences and over-complicating business operations. Law number ten: "Simplicity is about subtracting the obvious, and adding the meaningful."

MARKETING AESTHETICS, Bernd H. Schmitt, Alex Simonson (Free Press, 1997). In this precursor to **EXPERIENTIAL MARKETING**, Schmitt and Simonson take Aaker's thesis one step further by showing that aesthetics is what drives emotion. What makes a brand irresistible? What styles and themes are needed for different contexts? What meanings do symbols convey? The answers to these questions are crucial for inspiring organic loyalty in customers.

COLLABORATION

CREATING THE PERFECT DESIGN BRIEF, Peter L. Phillips (Alworth Press, 2004). Here's a practical guide to getting all your collaborators on the same page—literally. Unless you can clearly delineate goals and roles, your collaborative project is doomed to mediocrity or even failure. Any design manager intent on building an internal design department or a creative metateam would do well to incorporate Phillips's thinking into its management system.

THE FIFTH DISCIPLINE, Peter M. Senge (Currency, 1994). Senge brought systems thinking—what he terms the fifth discipline—to the business management dialogue. Other disciplines include personal mastery and team learning. He encourages employees and managers to examine the mental models that at first allow organizations to codify their successes and later keep them from evolving with the market. Senge offers his own mental models, based on archetypal systemsthinking, to help companies look at their businesses holistically.

ORGANIZING GENIUS, Warren Bennis and Patricia Ward Biederman (Perseus Publishing, 1998). An expert on leadership skills, Bennis shows how to unleash the creative potential of teamwork within the organization. A seminal work on the subject, and highly inspirational.

PRESENTATION ZEN, Garr Reynolds (New Riders, 2008). If a business is a decision factory, then the presentations that inform those decisions play a huge part in the quality of those decisions. If you're merely piling fact upon fact, bullet point upon bullet point, you're missing out on the full power of persuasion. Author Reynolds shows you how to think through your story, consciously apply the principles of design, and keep it very, very simple.

SERIOUS PLAY, Michael Schrage (Harvard Business School Press, 1999). Schrage isn't kidding—he seriously wants you to adopt a collaborative model. He says the secret is building quick-and-dirty prototypes, which serve as shared spaces for innovation. He brings the reader into the wild world of the right brain, where play equals seriousness, and serious players work on fun-loving teams.

SIX THINKING HATS, Edward de Bono (Little, Brown and Company, 1985). When executives try to brainstorm the future of their organization, the discussion can quickly turn to confusion and disagreement. Edward de Bono, acknowledged master of thinking skills, shows how to get the group's best ideas by focusing on one kind thinking at a time. By organizing the session into a series of "hats", i.e., red for emotions, black for devil's advocate, green for creativity, ideas aren't shot down before they're proposed.

THE TEN FACES OF INNOVATION, Tom Kelley (Doubleday, 2005). Kelley, from design mega-firm IDEO, maintains that the idea-killing power of the "devil's advocate" is so strong that it takes up to ten innovation protagonists to subdue him. He offers the "anthropologist," who goes into the field to see how customers really live; the "cross-pollinator," who connects ideas, people, and technology in new ways; and the "hurdler," who leaps tall obstacles that block innovation.

UNSTUCK, Keith Yamashita and Sandra Spataro, Ph.D. (Portfolio, 2004). When all else fails, get **UNSTUCK**. This little book from a founder of Stone Yamashita Partners and a professor of organizational behavior is chock full of tips and tricks for improving collaboration. The authors couple a highly visual communication style with bite-size ideas (not unlike **THE DESIGNFUL COMPANY**), to create a fun, easy tool for jumpstarting your team. More inspirational than instructional, it allows the reader to participate in the process.

Neutron is a San Francisco firm whose stated mission is "to incite business revolution by unleashing the power of creative process." Ambitious? Maybe. Dangerous? Absolutely. Every day we do battle in the gap between the "deciding" mode of the past and the "designing" mode of the future. The ideas in THE DESIGNFUL COMPANY are the same ideas that drive us crazy at night, divert us in our morning shower, and distract us on our daily commute.

As you might imagine, Neutron associates tend to defy tidy classification. Rather than strategists, program managers, and facilitators, for example, our ranks are filled with change agents, creative catalysts, and epiphany engineers. No one has a normal job description; no one wears a single hat. Strategists write, designers think, writers design, researchers teach, and everyone learns from everyone. The only common thread is a passion for improving the way business does business by injecting the process of design.

When we launched Neutron in 2003, our work was focused on redefining branding. Branding was—and still is—commonly confused with advertising, corporate identity, and public relations. I wrote my first book THE BRAND GAP to fix this misconception, explaining that a company's brand is not about communication but reputation. In other words, it's not what YOU say it is. It's what THEY say it is. In world where customers have too many choices, and where products can be commoditized overnight, a company's brand is both its connection with customers and a barrier to competition.

But brands are only as good as the skills that build them. Today our work is focused on culture-change activities as well—strategies and tactics that build designful companies. In practical terms, this may require a three-year engagement that includes transformation planning, training programs, innovation labs, skilling workshops, team facilitation, and other levers of change. Or it may take little more than a one-day strategy intervention to make a tangible difference. At any level of involvement, Neutron's role is essentially the same: We build the teams that build the brands

If you've ever worked in a company where process overshadows purpose; where colleagues don't collaborate; where decisions seem disconnected; where brand expressions get lost in translation; where the spark of inspiration fizzles before it reaches the customer; or where it's just no fun to come to the office, you've experienced the uncomfortable gap between the "deciding" mode of the past and the "designing" mode of the future. This is the gap that Neutron is helping to bridge.

Learn more at www.neutronllc.com.

ABOUT THE AUTHOR

Marty Neumeier is president of Neutron, a San Francisco firm that designs and facilitates culture-change programs that spur innovation, build charismatic brands, and unleash organizational creativity.

Neumeier began his career as a designer, but soon added writing and strategy to his repertoire, working variously as an identity designer, art director, copywriter, journalist, package designer, magazine publisher, and brand consultant. By the mid-1990s he had developed hundreds of brand icons, retail packages, and other communications for companies such as Apple Computer, Adobe Systems, Netscape Communications, Eastman Kodak, and Hewlett-Packard.

In 1996 he launched CRITIQUE, the magazine of design thinking, which quickly became the leading forum for improving design effectiveness through critical analysis. In editing CRITIQUE, Neumeier joined the growing conversation about bridging the gap between business strategy and customer experience, which led directly to the formation of Neutron and the ideas in his series of "whiteboard overview" books.

Neumeier divides his professional time among three activities—managing Neutron, writing books and articles on business and design, and facilitating workshops on innovation. Outside of work he enjoys cooking, movies, reading, and traveling. While he and his wife spend most of the year in Palo Alto, California, they make regular sojourns to the southwest of France where they own a small farmhouse in need of "nonstop renovation."